Genealogy of Duncan, Dunkart, McCloud, Layman, Oberlander, Reiman, Gipe, Klein, Warner, Neal, Surr, Baugher, Miller, Neipp, Kepner, Hamm, Deitz et al

Thompson Family History v. 3 of Rhineland-Palatinate, Saarland & Prussia, Germany; and Northumberland, Centre, Philadelphia, Lancaster & York Counties, PA

MARC D. THOMPSON

Family histories require constant revision. As this century moves along, more and more information becomes digitally or electronically disposable. If we do not save this information, it may be lost forever. Please contact author with any corrections or additions, marc@VirtuFit.net.

ISBN: 978-0-9883440-2-0

Photography by Marc D. Thompson

MARC D. THOMPSON - VIRTUFIT.NET®
www.VirtuFit.net - marc@VirtuFit.net
Skype: VirtuFit
Ideafit: www.ideafit.com/profile/marc-d-thompson

Also by Author

Genealogy of Anderson, Keefer, Gaugler, Livezly…,
https://www.createspace.com/4548631, © 2014, 978-0-9883440-3-7

Genealogy of Batdorf, Wert, Peters, Row…,
https://www.createspace.com/4530376, © 2013, 978-0-9883440-1-3

Genealogy of Thompson, Hensel, Goodman, Updegrove…,
https://www.createspace.com/4530098, © 2013, 978-0-9883440-4-4

Virtual Personal Training Manual, © 2013, 978-0-9883440-9-9,
https://www.createspace.com/4428594

Poems...Of Eternal Moments, © 2012, 978-0-9883440-8-2,
https://www.createspace.com/3905443

The Fitness Book of Lists, © 2012, 978-0-6156563-0-4,
https://www.createspace.com/4007866

Genealogy of Romano, Disimone, Vitale, Viviano..., © 2012,
978-0-9883440-6-8, https://www.createspace.com/4011878

Fitness Quotes of Humorous Inspiration, © 2011, 978-0-9883440-8-2,
https://www.createspace.com/4052242,

Genealogy of Wittle, Acri, Stewart, Barbuscio..., © 2011,
978-0-988-3440-5-1, https://www.createspace.com/4040063

Genealogy of Mazo, Curry, Thompson, Mason..., © 2010,
978-0-988-3440-7-5, https://www.createspace.com/4005580

Thompson Family History, © 2010, 978-0-9883440-4-4

Dedication

This book is fondly dedicated

to my loving sisters,

Tory St. Thompson Shannon

&

Jill D. Thompson.

Foreword

by Stephany Duncan Gormley

Marc Thompson labored for decades to provide his nuclear and extended family members (including cousins like me) with this incredibly detailed volume of family history. The pages contain all of the requisite dates, names, and places that one expects from genealogical research. Beyond these facts, its subtext harbors Marc's transcendental journey into each branch of the families represented. It is also a living manuscript that Marc hopes will evolve as new generations or contemporary extended family members not yet known to him leaf through its pages and add their names to the branches of the family tree or add some knowledge that may have not been discovered at the time of its publication.

The ultimate gift of any family history is the realization of the intimate and deeply personal connection we have with each measure of our ancestry. As Walt Whitman wrote:

With antecedents;

With my fathers and mothers, and the accumulations of past ages;

With all of which, had it not been, I would not be here, as I am

--From "With Antecedents"

Marc's passion and the compilation of his skillful work in this volume provides that gift to everyone who finds all or part of their family's past in its pages. I thank him for giving me that gift and I hope that current and future generations of readers of his work will appreciate his wonderful gift as well.

Preface

Our 30 years journey of knowledge has led to a plethora of information. We have learned much. We have discovered our roots, good and bad. It has molded us. We have found we are related to some famous and infamous folks and there are some areas of the country that are named for our distant families.

We are direct-line descendants of King Philip of France and the Royal families Cleves. We are descended from Civil War servicemen Elijah Anderson, Thomas E. Batdorf, Andrew G. Hensel, Daniel Updegrove, John H. Wert, Louis L. Stewart and Jacob Wittle, War of 1812 servicemen Adam Frantz and Andrew Hensel, and Revolutionary War servicemen William Anderson, John Daniel Angst, Philip Jacob Bordner, Peter Brown (British), John Faber, Casper Hensel, John George Herrold, Jacob Lehman, Michael Leymon, Andrew Messerschmidt, John Miller, John Balthaser Romberger, Jonas Rudy, John George Schupp, John Peter Shaffer, John George Felten and Gottleib Zink. Our ties also include European Mayors John Guerne and John Emmerich, religious leaders John Peter Batdorf, John Batdorf, John George Bager Jr., John George Bager Sr., John Heilferich Lotz , George Gaukel and Entrepreneur Alexander Thompson.

We are direct-line descendants of the some famous homesteads and locations, including the George Bager Homestead, Abbottstown, PA, the Chris Miller Homestead, North Lebanon Township, PA, the George Mennig (Minnich) Homestead, PA,the Thomas Benfield homestead, Berks Co., PA, the Livesey Homestead, Philadelphia, PA, and the Wirth Homestead, Lykens Valley Golf Course, Dauphin Co., PA (demolished 1989). Additionally, our ancestor's names were immortalized at these locations: Bordnersville, Kelly crossroads, Livesey Street, Herrold's

Island, Keefer's Station, Deibler's Gap, Deibler's Dam, Shoemakertown, all in Pennsylvania. Finally, our ancestors had surnames named after the Jura Mountains of Switzerland and Acri, Italy, among other locations.

We are collateral descendants of Presidents Dwight D. Eisenhower and William McKinley and Pennsylvania politicians Samuel Pennypacker, John Morton and Jonas Row. Civil War Brigadier General Galushia Pennypacker, Entertainers Marlon Brando, Les Brown and Ray W Brown, Religious leaders Conrad Weiser and Michael Enderline, Melba Dodge, Jesse Runkle, Enrico Caruso and Galla Curci are all cousins. Lastly, Taylor Wittel lists relations to James Madison, Zachary Taylor, Jefferson Davis and Gene Autry

This volume will serve to honor us with the researched and documented information of our background. Our ancestry was derived from this data, the Thompson Family History (TFH) genealogy, that includes:

This volume will serve to honor us with the researched and documented information of
our background. Our ancestry was derived from this data, the Thompson Family History (TFH)
genealogy, that includes:

7,633 Relatives in TFH
2,101 Marriages in TFH
1,274 Places in TFH
1,162 Sources (over 5,000 Sources not producing information) for TFH
1,107 Surnames in TFH
360 Media in TFH
20 Generations (12 Generations in format) in TFH
95 Age of oldest ancestor at death, Sarah E Wirt & Mrs. M. Curcio
89 Ancestors named John or Albert
85 Ancestors named same male name, John, Johannes, Jean, etc
82 Ancestors names Sophia (4) or Maria (78)
74 Ancestors named same female name, Mary, Maria, Mary Ann, etc.
51 Ancestors named Dolores or Ann
50 Most variations for single surname, Batdorf, Bodorff, Buderff, Pottorf, etc.
38 Ancestors named Mary or Frances

34 Ancestors named Shirley or Mary

27 Number of letters of longest female ancestor's name, Amelia Dorothy Elizabeth Bager

24 Number of letters of longest male ancestor's name, Howard Andrew Carson Hensel

22 Age of youngest ancestor at death, Andrew Morton & Henry Rudin

21 Ancestors named Connor (1) or Adam (20)

17 Ancestors named Andrew (16) or Roman (1)

16 Youngest age when first child born, Myrtle A. Thompson & Fortune Marsico

13 Ancestors named Mary Ann

11 Number of countries ancestors born, DEU, ITA, IRL, SCO, ENG, FIN, SWE, CHE, FRA, HOL, PRT

7 Most different ancestral lines with same surname, Miller, Mueller, etc.

6 Number of states ancestors born in, PA, NY, DE, GA, SC, VA

5 Ancestors named Tyler (1) or Anthony (4)

5 Ancestors named Tiffany (1) or Rachel (4)

4 Ancestors named Paul or Paolo

4 Ancestors named Ed or Edward

3 Ancestors who died at sea, N. Benesch, G. Rieth & G. Shoemaker

2 Ancestors named Ashley (1) or Renae (1)

1 Ancestors named Gerald or Gilbert

45% relatives born in Pennsylvania

17% relatives born in Germany

14% relatives born in Scotland

9% relatives born in Italy

4% relatives born in Georgia

4% relatives born in South Carolina

4% relatives born in Ireland

2% relatives born in New York

1% relatives born in Virginia, Florida, Switzerland, England, Bohemia, France, Sweden, Finland & West Indies

Acknowledgments

Thanks to my parents without whom I wouldn't exist, and hence their parents, ad infinitum. Thanks to my sisters, for being there for me and showing interest in our history. Thanks to Joe who tutored me as a teen at the Pennsylvania State Library Genealogy room. Thanks to my hundreds of cousins, close and distant, that have selflessly donated their hard–worked family history to me. Thanks to every clerk and registrar, cemetery manager and LDS employee, who has taken their time to assist me discover our roots. This book is truly the love of thousands, both literally, my family, and figuratively, everyone else who selflessly helped.

Table Of Contents

Introduction

Genealogy was created in order for people to know the history of their lineage; to discover their origins; to prove bloodlines and royalty. Responding to their deep desire to understand and discover their past, this volume was compiled. It shall stand as part of the legacy of their ancestry.

Our mission is to document and record all that is available for our direct line and reap the enjoyment that this discovery brings. The first goal of the Thompson Family History (TFH) was to amass photographs of as many ancestors as possible. As a face can tell a thousand tales, so much can be learned from them. The second goal of the TFH was to document the medical background of our ancestors, so our children can lead a healthier life. The third goal of the TFH is to amass documentation of our ancestors in order to extend the lineage and to lead to information about the personality (biography) of our forefathers. Our ancestors are not a mere name. They have tales to tell, journeys to documents. They have accomplishments and set-backs. They have remembrances. They have goals, glories, and personalities. The Irish Kings would orally pass down their regal history. They would recite a list of names, their kin, noting outstanding events associated with the forbearers. The ancient Scottish bards similarly memorized their royal family, reciting the pedigrees of the Old Scot's Kings, regardless of the complexity.

Genealogy is a duty. The day we bear children, we took the responsibility of passing along our history. We are responsible for the knowledge of their grandparents and all the wisdom that comes with this knowledge. Our duty, then, includes our children's heritage, the names and faces of their forefathers and mothers. The medical history and genetic backgrounds of their blood lines; the Princes and the paupers; the photographs and historical areas and properties; the tragedies and joys. This TFH is our heritage and with this information we can be proud of ourselves, our past and aim toward a bright future and better lives. If our duty is neglected, as each generation passes, so will our family history.

Most genealogies tend to trace a descendancy or the paternal line (single ascendancy). Our purpose was to trace all ancestors with equal perseverance. This is a monumental, if not impossible, task. We have compiled a pedigree, beginning with our children and using an ahnentafel format. Our children are generation 1, their parents are generation 2, their grandparents are generation 3, etc. There is a family group sheet for each pair of parents along the pedigree. The emphasis at present is on generations 1 through 10, although we have researched as far back as generation 20. Additional collateral ancestors have begun to be added as of 2005. In most cases, the Anglicized first an middle name were used throughout the TFH. For example, Johann Heinrich is John Henry and Orsala Francesca is Ursula Frances. The most commonly found surname was used, whether Anglicized or not. The majority of the collateral information was derived from the US census records. To preserve privacy, all information on living persons has been removed or privatized.

As genealogists will agree, no family history is 100% accurate. We have made errors as others have before us. As this century moves along, more and more information becomes digitally or electronically disposable. If we do not save this information, it may be lost forever. The TFH is a guide for future generations who may use this information for their own goals, whatever they maybe. We have given our children a foundation. Take it, improve it, embrace it.

The continued excellence of this genealogy will be improved by the following plan.

A. Correct errors and complete Source Citations.

B. Collect photographs and medical history of ancestors.

D. Document more personal information of ancestors leading to a more biographical history of family.

E. Expound on current family group sheets and extend parentage.

F. Begin a written biographical volumes (Narratives)

I have a desire and I have a bond. I have a desire to know from whence we came. I want to know our history, our origins. I want to know what our ancestors did, how they persevered and how the spark of life made it way from Geoffrey Livesay born 1410 in England to Sophia born 2004 in Florida. I feel a bond. I have a strong connection to the late 19th century.

If I were given the opportunity to live in any era, I most certainly would pick the 1860-1880's. The time was simple and the people were honest. People worked hard and took pride in their family, their home and their reputation. When I look into the eyes of our ancestors from this time period, I feel a link. I would have fit nicely in their time. Read and enjoy.

Marc D. Thompson

Chapter One

Our family's pedigree and history.

Our ancestors and their family history, with details of life and times of all of our relatives, including cited sources.

Pedigree Chart

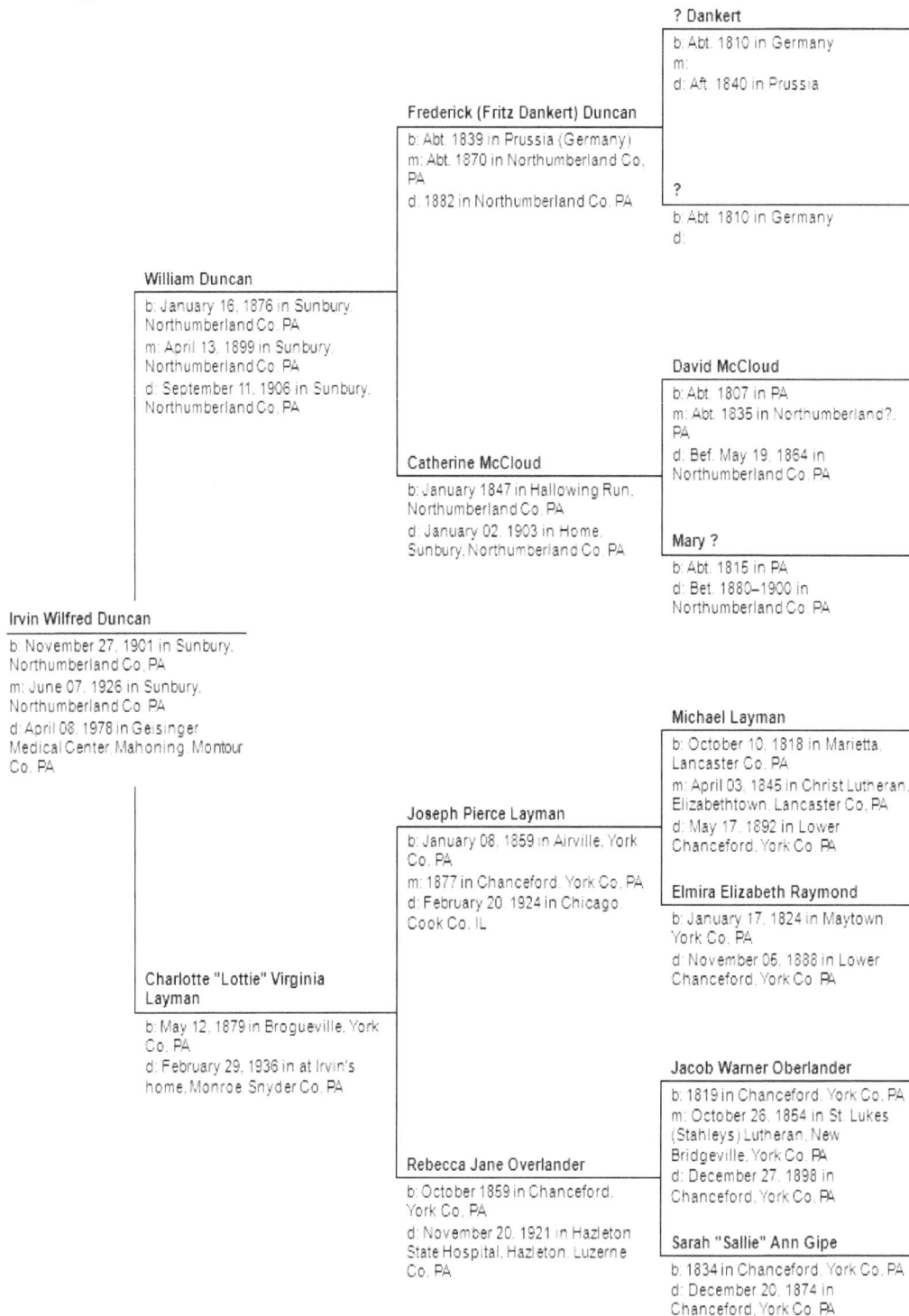

? Dankert
b: Abt. 1810 in Germany
m:
d: Aft. 1840 in Prussia

Frederick (Fritz Dankert) Duncan
b: Abt. 1839 in Prussia (Germany)
m: Abt. 1870 in Northumberland Co,
PA
d: 1882 in Northumberland Co. PA

?
b: Abt. 1810 in Germany
d:

William Duncan
b: January 16, 1876 in Sunbury,
Northumberland Co. PA
m: April 13, 1899 in Sunbury,
Northumberland Co. PA
d: September 11, 1906 in Sunbury,
Northumberland Co. PA

David McCloud
b: Abt. 1807 in PA
m: Abt. 1835 in Northumberland?,
PA
d: Bef. May 19, 1864 in
Northumberland Co. PA

Catherine McCloud
b: January 1847 in Hallowing Run,
Northumberland Co. PA
d: January 02, 1903 in Home,
Sunbury, Northumberland Co. PA

Mary ?
b: Abt. 1815 in PA
d: Bet. 1880–1900 in
Northumberland Co. PA

Irvin Wilfred Duncan
b: November 27, 1901 in Sunbury,
Northumberland Co. PA
m: June 07, 1926 in Sunbury,
Northumberland Co. PA
d: April 08, 1978 in Geisinger
Medical Center, Mahoning, Montour
Co. PA

Michael Layman
b: October 10, 1818 in Marietta,
Lancaster Co. PA
m: April 03, 1845 in Christ Lutheran,
Elizabethtown, Lancaster Co. PA
d: May 17, 1892 in Lower
Chanceford, York Co. PA

Joseph Pierce Layman
b: January 08, 1859 in Airville, York
Co. PA
m: 1877 in Chanceford, York Co. PA
d: February 20, 1924 in Chicago,
Cook Co. IL

Elmira Elizabeth Raymond
b: January 17, 1824 in Maytown,
York Co. PA
d: November 05, 1888 in Lower
Chanceford, York Co. PA

**Charlotte "Lottie" Virginia
Layman**
b: May 12, 1879 in Brogueville, York
Co. PA
d: February 29, 1936 in at Irvin's
home, Monroe, Snyder Co. PA

Jacob Warner Oberlander
b: 1819 in Chanceford, York Co. PA
m: October 26, 1854 in St. Lukes
(Stahleys) Lutheran, New
Bridgeville, York Co. PA
d: December 27, 1898 in
Chanceford, York Co. PA

Rebecca Jane Overlander
b: October 1859 in Chanceford,
York Co. PA
d: November 20, 1921 in Hazleton
State Hospital, Hazleton, Luzerne
Co. PA

Sarah "Sallie" Ann Gipe
b: 1834 in Chanceford, York Co. PA
d: December 20, 1874 in
Chanceford, York Co. PA

6

Descendants

1 Irvin Wilfred Duncan b: November 27, 1901 in Sunbury, Northumberland Co, PA, d: April 08, 1978 in Geisinger Medical Center, Mahoning, Montour Co, PA

... + Mary "Mamie" Lucetta Anderson b: April 11, 1908 in At home, Sunbury, Northumberland Co, PA, m: June 07, 1926 in Sunbury, Northumberland Co, PA, d: April 03, 1989 in Derry, Montour Co, PA

......2 Charlotte E Duncan b: December 04, 1926 in PA, d: 1926

......2 Ethel L Duncan b: December 04, 1926 in PA, d: 2011

...... + Living Cameron

.........3 Living Cameron

.........3 Living Cameron

.... + Patricia ?

.... + Debra ?

.........3 Living Cameron

.... + Richard Smith

.........3 Living Cameron

.... + Michael Hampton

.... + James Wolfe

......2 Living Duncan

...... + Living Newberry

.........3 Living Duncan

.... + Ann Philips

.........3 Living Duncan

.... + Gene Gormley

.........3 Living Duncan

.... + Jeffrey Davis

.... + Dominick Silla

.... + Manfred Klatt

...... + Living James

...... + Living ?

......2 Living Duncan

...... + Living Zeigler

.........3 Living Zeigler

.... + Kathy Loeffler

.........3 Living Zeigler

.... + L Williams

.........3 Living Zeigler

.... + D A Clark

.........3 Living Zeigler

.... + J Renard

......2 Ralph Richard Duncan b: 1934 in PA, d: 1934

......2 Living Duncan

...... + Living Thompson

.........3 Living St. Thompson

.... + Living ?

.........3 Living Thompson

.... + Living ?

.........3 Living Thompson

.... + Melvalean Curry b: January 15, 1967 in Jefferson, Philadelphia Co, PA, d: May 28, 2008 in Boynton Beach, Palm Beach, Florida, USA

.... + Living Wittle

....   + Living Romano
......2 Living Duncan
......   + Living Drendall
.........3 Living Duncan
....   + A ?

Family History

Generation 1

1. **Irvin Wilfred Duncan** (son of William Duncan and Charlotte "Lottie" Virginia Layman) was born on November 27, 1901 in Sunbury, Northumberland Co, PA[1, 2, 3]. He died on April 08, 1978 in Geisinger Medical Center, Mahoning, Montour Co, PA[1, 4, 5]. He married **Mary "Mamie" Lucetta Anderson** (daughter of William Morris Anderson and Emma Louisa Keefer) on June 07, 1926 in Sunbury, Northumberland Co, PA. She was born on April 11, 1908 in At home, Sunbury, Northumberland Co, PA[6, 7, 8, 9]. She died on April 03, 1989 in Derry, Montour Co, PA[1, 7, 8, 10].

More About Irvin Wilfred Duncan:
Burial: April 11, 1978 in Pomfret Manor Cemetery, Sunbury, Northumberland Co, PA[1, 5, 11]
Cause Of Death: ; Squamous cell carcinoma of lung w/pulmonary edema w/ASCVD.[5]
Census: 1910 in Sunbury, Northumberland Co, PA[12]
Census: 1920 in Sunbury, Northumberland Co, PA[13]
Census: 1930
Education: 1910 ; School[14]
Education: 1920 ; School[15]
Medical Condition: ; lung cancer due to pulmonary edema and arteriosclerosis,
lung cancer, heart disease, hypertension, varicose, veins
Funeral: April 11, 1978 in M. Quay Olley [Olley-Gotlob] Funeral Home, 539 Race St., Sunbury, Northumberland Co, PA[5]
Occupation: Abt. 1940 ; Produce Store Owner (Sunbury, Hummels Wharf)[1]
Occupation: 1978 ; Fruit & Produce[5]
Political Party: Republican
Religion: ; Lutheran[1]
Religion: ; United Methodist[16]
Residence: 1901 in Susquehanna Ave., Sunbury, Northumberland Co, PA[3]
Residence: 1910 in 63 8th St., Sunbury, Northumbelrand, PA[14]
Residence: 1920 in 920 Susquehanna Ave., Sunbury, Northumberland Co, PA[15]
Residence: 1963 in Sunbury, Northumberland Co, PA[17]

Residence: 1978 in RD 2, Selinsgrove, Snyder, PA 17870[5]
Residence: 1978 in Blue Hill, Dogtown, Jackson, Kantz, Kratzerville, Penn Avon, Salem, Selinsgrove, Verdilla, all Snyder, PA[4]
Social Security Number: 1978 ; 209-24-9584[4, 5]
Member: Hummels Wharf Fire Co, Finanacial & recording Sec., Rescue Hose Co Sby.[18]

Notes for Irvin Wilfred Duncan:
Have Photograph.

Middle name also Francis.

Unsure if he passed at someone's home or at the Medical Center. Died Selinsgrove, Sunbury [Duncan family information, Jack Lehman, North Charleston, SC]

More About Mary "Mamie" Lucetta Anderson:
Burial: April 05, 1989 in Pomfret Manor Cemetery, Sunbury, Northumberland Co, PA[1, 8, 19]
Cause Of Death: ; Carcinoma of lung w/ metastasis[8]
Census: 1910 in Sunbury, Northumberland Co, PA[20]
Census: 1920 in Monroe, Snyder Co, PA[21]
Census: 1930
Education: 1920 ; School[22]
Medical Condition: ; lung cancer metastasis, hypertension, lung cancer, stroke
Funeral: 1989 in VL Seebold, 601 N High St, Selinsgrove, Snyder Co, PA[8]
Occupation: Abt. 1930 ; Domestic cook[1]
Occupation: Abt. 1935 ; Silk Mill
Political Party: Democrat
Probate: February 05, 1990 in Montour Co, PA[10]
Religion: ; Lutheran[1]
Residence: Bet. 1969-1970 in Sunbury, Northumberland Co, PA[23]
Residence: 1989 in RD 2, Box 574, Danville, Mountour, PA 17821[24]
Social Security Number: 1989 ; 170-26-9870[1, 7, 25]

Notes for Mary "Mamie" Lucetta Anderson:
Have Photograph.

Mamie was named for her grandmother, Lucetta Gaugler [author,1990]

Born Jackson or Kratzerville, Snyder Co, PA [Duncan family information, Jack Lehman, North Charleston, SC]

Generation 2

2.   **William Duncan** (son of Frederick (Fritz Dankert) Duncan and Catherine McCloud) was born on January 16, 1876 in Sunbury, Northumberland Co, PA[26, 27, 28]. He died on September 11, 1906 in Sunbury, Northumberland Co, PA[27]. He married **Charlotte "Lottie" Virginia Layman** (daughter of Joseph Pierce Layman and Rebecca Jane Overlander) on April 13, 1899 in Sunbury, Northumberland Co, PA[28, 29, 30].

3.   **Charlotte "Lottie" Virginia Layman** (daughter of Joseph Pierce Layman and Rebecca Jane Overlander) was born on May 12, 1879 in Brogueville, York Co, PA[31, 32]. She died on February 29, 1936 in at Irvin's home, Monroe, Snyder Co, PA[32].

More About William Duncan:
b: January 18, 1876 in Sunbury, Northumberland Co, PA[33]
Baptism: September 29, 1876 in Zion Evangelical Lutheran Church, Sunbury, Northumberland Co, PA[34, 35]
Burial: September 14, 1906 in Pomfret Manor Cemetery, Sunbury, Northumberland Co, PA[36, 37]
Cause Of Death: ; Pulmonary tuberculosis[27]
Census: 1880 in Sunbury, Northumberland Co, PA[38]
Census: 1900 in Sunbury, Northumberland Co, PA[39]
Funeral: 1906 in J. Hartman, Sunbury, Northumberland Co, PA[27]
Occupation: 1899 ; Blacksmith helper[31]
Occupation: 1900 ; Blacksmith[39]
Occupation: 1901 ; Laborer[40]
Occupation: 1906 ; Machinist[27]
Occupation: ; Railroad
Probate: September 17, 1906 in Sunbury, Northumberland Co, PA[41]
Residence: 1899 in Sunbury, Northumberland Co, PA[31]
Residence: 1900 in 929 Railroad Ave., Sunbury, Northumberland Co, PA[39]

Residence: 1901 in 918 Susquehanna Ave., Sunbury, Northumberland, PA[40]
Residence: 1906 in 920 Susquehanna Ave., Sunbury, Northumberland Co, PA[27]
Will: July 24, 1906 in Sunbury, Northumberland Co, PA[41]

Notes for William Duncan:
Have Photograph.

Find Harris' relationship to William (not his son).

More About Charlotte "Lottie" Virginia Layman:
b: May 1880[42]
b: May 12, 1881[43]
Burial: March 03, 1936 in Pomfret Manor Cemetery, Sunbury, Northumberland Co, PA[32, 44]
Cause Of Death: ; Cerebral hemorrhage w/interstitial nephritis[45]
Census: 1880
Census: 1900 in Sunbury, Northumberland Co, PA
Census: 1910 in Sunbury, Northumberland Co, PA[12]
Census: 1920 in Sunbury, Northumberland Co, PA (Willard)[13]
Census: 1930 in Sunbury, Northumberland Co, PA (Willard)[46]
Funeral: 1936 in F.K. Sutton, Selinsgrove, Snyder Co, PA[47]
Occupation: 1900 ; Own income[14]
Occupation: 1936 ; Retired[32]
Residence: 1899 in Sunbury, Northumberland Co, PA[31]
Residence: 1910 in 63 8th St., Sunbury, Northumberland Co, PA[14]
Residence: Bet. 1920-1930 in 920 Susquehanna Ave., Sunbury, Northumberland Co, PA[15, 48]

Notes for Charlotte "Lottie" Virginia Layman:
Have Photograph.

Charlotte "Lottie" Virginia Layman and William Duncan had the following child:
1. i. Irvin Wilfred Duncan (son of William Duncan and Charlotte "Lottie" Virginia Layman) was born on November 27, 1901 in Sunbury, Northumberland Co, PA[1, 2, 3]. He died on April 08, 1978 in Geisinger Medical Center, Mahoning, Montour

Co, PA[1, 4, 5]. He married Mary "Mamie" Lucetta Anderson (daughter of William Morris Anderson and Emma Louisa Keefer) on June 07, 1926 in Sunbury, Northumberland Co, PA. She was born on April 11, 1908 in At home, Sunbury, Northumberland Co, PA[6, 7, 8, 9]. She died on April 03, 1989 in Derry, Montour Co, PA[1, 7, 8, 10].

Generation 3

4. **Frederick (Fritz Dankert) Duncan** (son of ? Dankert and ?) was born about Abt. 1839 in Prussia (Germany). He died in 1882 in Northumberland Co, PA. He married **Catherine McCloud** (daughter of David McCloud and Mary ?) about Abt. 1870 in Northumberland Co, PA.

5. **Catherine McCloud** (daughter of David McCloud and Mary ?) was born in January 1847 in Hallowing Run, Northumberland Co, PA[49]. She died on January 02, 1903 in Home, Sunbury, Northumberland Co, PA[49].

More About Frederick (Fritz Dankert) Duncan:
Burial: 1882 in Old Cemetery Sunbury, Northumberland Co, PA
Census: 1870 in Sunbury, Northumberland Co, PA[50]
Census: 1880 in Sunbury, Northumberland Co, PA[38]
Immigration: Abt. 1865
Occupation: Bet. 1870-1880 ; Laborer[51]
Property: 1870 in $500[52]
Residence: 1880 in Short St., Sunbury, Northumberland Co, PA[53]

Notes for Frederick (Fritz Dankert) Duncan:
Wife Sarah [1870 United States Census, Dungan household, Northumberland Co, PA, www.ancestry.com]

Donker: Dutch: nickname for someone with dark hair or a dark complexion, from Middle Dutch donker, donkel 'dark'. Dunker, Duncan: North German: nickname from Middle Low German dunker 'dark', 'conceited', or 'unclear'. Dankert means 'strong-willed.'

More About Catherine McCloud:
b: March 05, 1849 in PA[54]

Burial: January 06, 1903 in Old Sunbury Cemetery, Sunbury, Northumberland Co, PA[49]
Cause Of Death: ; Dropsy (ie, Edema of kidney) w/heart disease
Census: 1850 in Lower Augusta, Northumberland Co, PA
Census: 1860 in Sunbury, Northumberland Co, PA (Mary)[55]
Census: 1870
Census: 1880 in Sunbury, Northumberland Co, PA
Census: 1900 in Sunbury, Northumberland Co, PA[39]
Occupation: Abt. 1870 ; Servant
Occupation: 1880 ; Keeping house[56]
Occupation: 1900 ; Day laborer[39]
Residence: 1900 in 927 Railroad Ave., Sunbury, Northumberland Co, PA[39]
Residence: 1903 in 1014 R.R. Ave., Sunbury, Northumberland Co, PA[49]

Catherine McCloud and Frederick (Fritz Dankert) Duncan had the following children:

    i.   Melinda E Duncan (daughter of Frederick (Fritz Dankert) Duncan and Catherine McCloud) was born on January 17, 1871 in Sunbury, Northumberland Co, PA[57]. She died on April 27, 1933 in Sunbury, Northumberland Co, PA[57]. She married Albert Geiser. He was born in 1870. He died in 1948.

    ii.   Sarah "Sallie" Duncan (daughter of Frederick (Fritz Dankert) Duncan and Catherine McCloud) was born on March 14, 1872 in Sunbury, Northumberland Co, PA[58, 59]. She died on February 03, 1915 in Sunbury, Northumberland Co, PA[58]. She married ?.

2.   iii.   William Duncan (son of Frederick (Fritz Dankert) Duncan and Catherine McCloud) was born on January 16, 1876 in Sunbury, Northumberland Co, PA[26, 27, 28]. He died on September 11, 1906 in Sunbury, Northumberland Co, PA[27]. He married Charlotte "Lottie" Virginia Layman (daughter of Joseph Pierce Layman and Rebecca Jane Overlander) on April 13, 1899 in Sunbury, Northumberland Co, PA[28, 29, 30]. She was born on May 12, 1879 in Brogueville, York Co, PA[31, 32]. She died on February 29, 1936 in at Irvin's home, Monroe, Snyder Co, PA[32].

    iv.   Gertrude "Gerty" Duncan (daughter of Frederick (Fritz

Dankert) Duncan and Catherine McCloud) was born on October 12, 1878 in Sunbury, Northumberland Co, PA.

v. Hannah Artila "Lilly" Duncan (daughter of Frederick (Fritz Dankert) Duncan and Catherine McCloud) was born on December 02, 1880 in Sunbury, Northumberland Co, PA[60]. She died after Aft. 1930. She married James F Kerstetter. He was born in October 1881 in PA. He died after Aft. 1930.

vi. Charles "Charley" Duncan (son of Frederick (Fritz Dankert) Duncan and Catherine McCloud) was born on June 26, 1882 in Sunbury, Northumberland Co, PA[61]. He died on February 12, 1924 in Sunbury, Northumberland Co, PA. He married Eula I Masteller (daughter of WD Masteller and Ervina A ?) in 1909. She was born in 1892 in PA. She died after Aft. 1930 in CA.

6. **Joseph Pierce Layman** (son of Michael Layman and Elmira Elizabeth Raymond) was born on January 08, 1859 in Airville, York Co, PA[1, 28, 32]. He died on February 20, 1924 in Chicago, Cook Co, IL[62, 63, 64]. He married **Rebecca Jane Overlander** (daughter of Jacob Warner Oberlander and Sarah "Sallie" Ann Gipe) in 1877 in Chanceford, York Co, PA[65].

7. **Rebecca Jane Overlander** (daughter of Jacob Warner Oberlander and Sarah "Sallie" Ann Gipe) was born in October 1859 in Chanceford, York Co, PA[1, 28]. She died on November 20, 1921 in Hazleton State Hospital, Hazleton, Luzerne Co, PA[28, 66].

More About Joseph Pierce Layman:
Burial: February 22, 1924 in Evergreen Cemetery, Chicago, IL[64, 67]
Cause Of Death: ; Valvular heart disease (aorotic) w/chronic nephritis & cystitis[64]
Census: 1860 in Lower Chanceford, York Co, PA[68]
Census: 1870 in Lower Chanceford, York Co, PA[69]
Census: 1880
Census: 1900 in Sunbury, Northumberland Co, PA (Laynon)[70]
Census: 1910
Census: 1920 in Chicago, Cook, IL[71]
Education: 1870 ; School[72]

Funeral: February 22, 1924 in JJ Sullivan[64]
Occupation: 1900 ; Brakeman (RR)[73]
Occupation: Abt. 1910 ; Engineer
Occupation: 1920 ; Store room (Packing House)[71]
Occupation: 1924 ; Stationary & Locomotive Engineer[64]
Religion: ; Methodist[1]
Residence: 1900 in 209 3rd St., Sunbury, Northumberland Co, PA[73]
Residence: 1920 in Blackstone Avenue, Chicago, Cook, IL[71]
Residence: 1924 in Chicago, Cook Co, IL[63]
Residence: 1924 in 908 W 70th St, Chicago, Cook Co, IL[64]

Notes for Joseph Pierce Layman:
Died 3/20/24 Chicago, IL, buried Evergreen Cemetery, Chicago, IL
[Duncan family information, Jack Lehman, North Charleston, SC &
Died 2/19/24 Leyman family information, source unknown]

More About Rebecca Jane Overlander:
Burial: November 23, 1921 in Pomfret Manor Cemetery, Sunbury,
Northumberland Co, PA[1, 66, 74]
Cause Of Death: ; Pneumonia, Labor[66]
Census: 1860
Census: 1870 in Chanceford, York Co, PA (Rebeck)[75]
Census: 1880
Census: 1900 in Sunbury, Northumberland Co, PA
Census: 1910 in Sunbury, Northumberland Co, PA (Laymer)[76]
Census: 1920 in Chicago, Cook, IL[71]
Education: 1870 ; School[77]
Funeral: 1921 in P? Manor, Weatherly, Carbon, PA[66]
Occupation: Abt. 1885 ; Homemaker
Religion: ; Methodist[1]
Residence: 1910 in 517 Chestnut St., Sunbury, Northumberland Co,
PA[78]
Residence: 1921 in Weatherly, Carbon, PA[66]

Notes for Rebecca Jane Overlander:
Have Photograph.

Died Hazelton, Carbon, PA [Duncan family information, Jack Lehman,
North Charleston, SC]

Rebecca Jane Overlander and Joseph Pierce Layman had the following children:

      i.   Lillian "Lillie" May Layman (daughter of Joseph Pierce Layman and Rebecca Jane Overlander) was born in 1878 in PA.

3.   ii.   Charlotte "Lottie" Virginia Layman (daughter of Joseph Pierce Layman and Rebecca Jane Overlander) was born on May 12, 1879 in Brogueville, York Co, PA[31, 32]. She died on February 29, 1936 in at Irvin's home, Monroe, Snyder Co, PA[32]. She married William Duncan (son of Frederick (Fritz Dankert) Duncan and Catherine McCloud) on April 13, 1899 in Sunbury, Northumberland Co, PA[28, 29, 30]. He was born on January 16, 1876 in Sunbury, Northumberland Co, PA[26, 27, 28]. He died on September 11, 1906 in Sunbury, Northumberland Co, PA[27]. She married William H McNutt (son of William McNutt) about Abt. 1910. He was born about Abt. 1887 in PA. She married William Grant Willard about Abt. 1920. He was born in 1874. He died in 1933.

      iii.   Earl William Layman (son of Joseph Pierce Layman and Rebecca Jane Overlander) was born about Abt. 1880 in PA.

      iv.   Living Layman (son of Joseph Pierce Layman and Rebecca Jane Overlander). He married Living Schuler.

      v.   Charles E Lehman (son of Joseph Pierce Layman and Rebecca Jane Overlander) was born in 1883 in PA. He married Dorothy Myers.

      vi.   Daniel Brunner Layman (son of Joseph Pierce Layman and Rebecca Jane Overlander) was born in 1884 in PA.

      vii.   Chester A Layman (son of Joseph Pierce Layman and Rebecca Jane Overlander) was born in August 1885 in PA.

      viii.   Theodore Augusta Layman (son of Joseph Pierce Layman and Rebecca Jane Overlander) was born in August 1886 in Columbia, Lancaster Co, PA. He married Frances ?. She was born in 1888 in PA.

ix. Joseph P Layman (son of Joseph Pierce Layman and Rebecca Jane Overlander) was born in 1887 in PA. He married Ida ?. She was born in 1887 in PA.

x. Mabel E Layman (daughter of Joseph Pierce Layman and Rebecca Jane Overlander) was born on May 18, 1892 in PA. She died in August 1974 in Harrisburg, Dauphin Co, PA. She married Ezra J Dodge. He was born about Abt. 1891 in PA.

xi. Margaret Edna Layman (daughter of Joseph Pierce Layman and Rebecca Jane Overlander) was born in 1893 in PA.

xii. Living Layman (son of Joseph Pierce Layman and Rebecca Jane Overlander). He married Living ?. He married Living ?.

xiii. Living Layman (son of Joseph Pierce Layman and Rebecca Jane Overlander). He married Living ?.

xiv Living Layman (daughter of Joseph Pierce Layman and Rebecca Jane Overlander).

Generation 4

8. **? Dankert** was born about Abt. 1810 in Germany. He died after Aft. 1840 in Prussia. He married **?**.

9. **?** was born about Abt. 1810 in Germany.

    ? and ? Dankert had the following child:

    4. i. Frederick (Fritz Dankert) Duncan (son of ? Dankert and ?) was born about Abt. 1839 in Prussia (Germany). He died in 1882 in Northumberland Co, PA. He married Catherine McCloud (daughter of David McCloud and Mary ?) about Abt. 1870 in Northumberland Co, PA. She was born in January 1847 in Hallowing Run, Northumberland Co, PA[49]. She died on January 02, 1903 in Home, Sunbury, Northumberland Co, PA[49]. He married Sarah ?.

10. **David McCloud** (son of John? McCloud) was born about Abt. 1807 in PA. He died before Bef. May 19, 1864 in Northumberland Co, PA[79]. He married **Mary ?** (daughter of ? and ?) about Abt. 1835 in

Northumberland?, PA.

11. **Mary ?** (daughter of ? and ?) was born about Abt. 1815 in PA. She died between 1880-1900 in Northumberland Co, PA.

More About David McCloud:
Census: 1810
Census: 1820
Census: 1830 in Augusta, Northumberland Co, PA
Census: 1840 in Augusta, Northumberland Co, PA
Census: 1850 in Lower Augusta, Northumberland Co, PA (Daniel Mcleod)[80]
Census: 1860 in Lower Augusta, Northumberland Co, PA[81]
Occupation: Bet. 1850-1860 ; Laborer[81, 82]
Occupation: ; Keeping house
Probate: May 19, 1864 in Lower Augusta, Northumberland Co, PA[79]
Property: 1850 in $100[82]
Property: 1860 in $100 + $40[83]

Notes for David McCloud:
Probable ancestor: Charity McCloud b1798 d1882, Lower Cem, Sunbury, PA

McCloud, McLeod: Scottish: variant of McLeod. Scottish: Anglicized form of Gaelic Mac Leòid, a patronymic from a Gaelic form of the Old Norse personal name Ljótr 'ugly'.

More About Mary ?:
Census: 1830 in husband; Augusta, Northumberland Co, PA w
Census: 1840 in husband; Augusta, Northumberland Co, PA w
Census: 1850 in Lower Augusta, Northumberland Co, PA
Census: 1860 in Lower Augusta, Northumberland Co, PA
Census: 1870 in Lower Augusta, Northumberland Co, PA[84]
Census: 1880 in Lower Augusta, Northumberland Co, PA[85]
Occupation: 1880 ; Keeping house[86]
Property: 1870 in $150 + $100[87]

Mary ? and David McCloud had the following children:
   i. Joseph McCloud (son of David McCloud and Mary ?) was

born in 1836 in PA. He married Mary Ann ?. She was born in 1840 in PA.

ii. Sarah McCloud (daughter of David McCloud and Mary ?) was born in 1839 in PA.

iii. Mary Ann McCloud (daughter of David McCloud and Mary ?) was born in 1844 in PA.

5.   iv. Catherine McCloud (daughter of David McCloud and Mary ?) was born in January 1847 in Hallowing Run, Northumberland Co, PA[49]. She died on January 02, 1903 in Home, Sunbury, Northumberland Co, PA[49]. She married Frederick (Fritz Dankert) Duncan (son of ? Dankert and ?) about Abt. 1870 in Northumberland Co, PA. He was born about Abt. 1839 in Prussia (Germany). He died in 1882 in Northumberland Co, PA.

v. Daniel McCloud (son of David McCloud and Mary ?) was born in 1849 in PA. He died on July 29, 1901 in Sunbury, Northumberland Co., PA. He married Mary Salome Reed. She was born in 1850 in PA. She died on July 03, 1900 in Sunbury, Northumberland Co., PA.

More About Mary Salome Reed:
Burial: 1900 in Pomfret

vi. Frederick McCloud (son of David McCloud and Mary ?) was born in 1852 in PA.

vii. Jeremiah "Jerry" McCloud (son of David McCloud and Mary ?) was born in 1853 in PA. He married Mary E Frye on October 11, 1890 in Sunbury, Northumberland Co, PA[88]. She was born in 1871 in PA.

viii. Judith McCloud (daughter of David McCloud and Mary ?) was born in 1855 in PA.

ix. William McCloud (son of David McCloud and Mary ?) was born in 1856 in PA.

12. **Michael Layman** (son of Michael Layman and Sarah Klein) was born on October 10, 1818 in Marietta, Lancaster Co, PA[1, 89]. He died on May 17, 1892 in Lower Chanceford, York Co, PA[1, 89]. He married **Elmira Elizabeth Raymond** (daughter of John Reiman and Nancy? ?) on April 03, 1845 in Christ Lutheran, Elizabethtown, Lancaster Co, PA[1].

13. **Elmira Elizabeth Raymond** (daughter of John Reiman and Nancy? ?) was born on January 17, 1824 in Maytown, York Co, PA[1]. She died on November 05, 1888 in Lower Chanceford, York Co, PA[1, 90].

More About Michael Layman:
Burial: May 1892 in Bethel United Methodist, Lower Chanceford, York Co, PA[1]
Census: 1820 in parents; w
Census: 1830 in parents; w
Census: 1840 in parents; w
Census: 1850 in Lower Chanceford, York Co, PA[91]
Census: 1860 in Lower Chanceford, York Co, PA[68]
Census: 1870 in Lower Chanceford, York Co, PA[92]
Census: 1880 in Lower Chanceford, York Co, PA[93]
Occupation: Abt. 1835 ; Farmer[92]
Occupation: Bet. 1850-1860 ; Boatman[91]
Occupation: 1870 ; Farmer[72]
Occupation: 1880 ; Lanlord (Landlord)[93]
Occupation: ; York Furnace
Occupation: ; Shenk's Ferry
Property: 1860 in $600 + $675[94]
Property: 1870 in $3000 + $2500[72]
Religion: ; Methodist[1]
Residence: 1847 in Relocated to York County[95]

Notes for Michael Layman:
MICHAEL LYMAN son of Michael and Sarah (Kline) Lyman, was born in Lancaster County, Penn., in 1823. His father was born in Centre County, and his mother in Lancaster County, Penn. Our subject remained in his native county until 1847, when he came to York County and entered the employ of the Tide Water Canal Company, and was located in Lower Chanceford Township. Here he continued to work for three years, and then began boating, which he continued

until 1870, when he removed to York Furnace and engaged in the hotel business. He remained there until 1884, when he removed to Shank's Ferry and entered the hotel business. Mr. Lyman was married in 1845, to Miss Elmira Raymond, of Dauphin County, Penn. They have seven children: Jacob, Eneas, Ella, Joseph, Charley, Lilly and Theodore. Mr. Lyman is a member of Lodge No. 125, of the Brotherhood of the Union. [History of York County, Pennsylvania. John Gibson, Historical Editor, Chicago: F. A. Battey Publishing Co., 1886]

Related to William McKinley, Jr. (January 29, 1843 - September 14, 1901) was the 25th President of the United States, and the last veteran of the American Civil War to be elected. By the 1880s, McKinley was a national Republican leader; his signature issue was high tariffs on imports as a formula for prosperity, as typified by his McKinley Tariff of 1890. As the Republican candidate in the 1896 presidential election, he upheld the gold standard, and promoted pluralism among ethnic groups. His campaign, designed by Mark Hanna, introduced new advertising-style campaign techniques that revolutionized campaign practices and beat back the crusading of his arch-rival, William Jennings Bryan. The 1896 election is often considered a realigning election that marked the beginning of the Progressive Era.[http://en.wikipedia.org/wiki/William_McKinley]

1) John McKinley 1728 & Margaret
…2) David McKinley 1755 & Anna Rose
……3) William McKinley
………4) Stephen McKinley bc1809 & Jane
…………5) William McKinley bc1835 & Margaret
……………6) Margaret J McKinley b1859 & Charles Layman
……3) James McKinley 1783
………4) William McKinley b1807 & Nancy Allison
…………5) William McKinley b1843 (President)

More About Elmira Elizabeth Raymond:
Burial: November 1888 in Bethel United Methodist, Lower Chanceford, York Co, PA[1, 90]
Census: 1830 in parents; w
Census: 1840 in parents; w
Census: 1850 in Lower Chanceford, York Co, PA
Census: 1860 in Lower Chanceford, York Co, PA

Census: 1870 in Lower Chanceford, York Co, PA[69]
Census: 1880 in Lower Chanceford, York Co, PA
Occupation: Bet. 1870-1880 ; Keeping house[72, 93]
Religion: ; Methodist[1]

Elmira Elizabeth Raymond and Michael Layman had the following children:

i. Jacob L Layman (son of Michael Layman and Elmira Elizabeth Raymond) was born in 1846 in PA. He died in 1911. He married Mary Elizabeth Bell. She was born in 1840.

ii. Sarah Layman (daughter of Michael Layman and Elmira Elizabeth Raymond) was born in 1847 in PA. She died about Abt. 1850.

iii. Uriah Layman (son of Michael Layman and Elmira Elizabeth Raymond) was born in 1848 in PA. He married Harriet "Hattie" McCleary. She was born in 1850.

iv. Mary E Layman (daughter of Michael Layman and Elmira Elizabeth Raymond) was born in 1849 in PA. She died about Abt. 1850.

v. Elmira "Ella" Layman (daughter of Michael Layman and Elmira Elizabeth Raymond) was born in 1853 in PA.

vi. Charles Gibbs Layman (son of Michael Layman and Elmira Elizabeth Raymond) was born in 1859 in PA. He married Margaret J McKinley. She was born in 1859 in PA.

Notes for Margaret J McKinley:
1) John McKinley 1728 & Margaret
...2) David McKinley 1755 & Anna Rose
......3) William McKinley
.........4) Stephen McKinley bc1809 & Jane
............5) William McKinley bc1835 & Margaret
...............6) Margaret J McKinley b1859 & Charles
Layman
......3) James McKinley 1783
.........4) William McKinley b1807 & Nancy Allison
............5) William McKinley b1843 (President)

6. vii. Joseph Pierce Layman (son of Michael Layman and Elmira Elizabeth Raymond) was born on January 08, 1859 in Airville, York Co, PA[1, 28, 32]. He died on February 20, 1924 in Chicago, Cook Co, IL[62, 63, 64]. He married Rebecca Jane Overlander (daughter of Jacob Warner Oberlander and Sarah "Sallie" Ann Gipe) in 1877 in Chanceford, York Co, PA[65]. She was born in October 1859 in Chanceford, York Co, PA[1, 28]. She died on November 20, 1921 in Hazleton State Hospital, Hazleton, Luzerne Co, PA[28, 66]. He married Mary ?. She was born in 1860.

viii. Lillian "Lillie" J Layman (daughter of Michael Layman and Elmira Elizabeth Raymond) was born in 1860 in PA. She died in 1894. She married Wesley J Ilges. He was born in 1850.

ix. Theodore A Layman (son of Michael Layman and Elmira Elizabeth Raymond) was born in 1862 in PA. He died in 1887. He married Phoebe A Hess. She was born in 1870.

14. **Jacob Warner Oberlander** (son of Michael Baugher Oberlander and Maria Catherine Warner) was born in 1819 in Chanceford, York Co, PA[1, 96]. He died on December 27, 1898 in Chanceford, York Co, PA[1, 96]. He married **Sarah "Sallie" Ann Gipe** (daughter of John Gipe and Elizabeth ?) on October 26, 1854 in St. Lukes (Stahleys) Lutheran, New Bridgeville, York Co, PA[1, 96, 97].

15. **Sarah "Sallie" Ann Gipe** (daughter of John Gipe and Elizabeth ?) was born in 1834 in Chanceford, York Co, PA[96]. She died on December 20, 1874 in Chanceford, York Co, PA[96, 98].

More About Jacob Warner Oberlander:
Burial: 1898
Census: 1820 in parents; w
Census: 1830 in father age 10; Upper Chanceford, York Co, PA w[99]
Census: 1840 in father age 10; Upper Chanceford, York Co, PA w[100]
Census: 1850 in Chanceford, York Co, PA[101]
Census: 1860 in Chanceford, York Co, PA[1, 102]
Census: 1870 in Chanceford, York Co, PA[103]
Census: 1880 in Chanceford, York Co, PA[1, 104]

Occupation: Bet. 1850-1880 ; Farmer[77, 105, 106, 107]
Property: 1860 in $4000 + $640[106]
Property: 1870 in $4000 + $1500[77]
Religion: ; Lutheran[1]

More About Sarah "Sallie" Ann Gipe:
Burial: December 1874 in St. Lukes (Stahleys) Lutheran, New
Bridgeville, York Co, PA[96]
Census: 1840 in parents; w
Census: 1850 in parents; w
Census: 1860 in Chanceford, York Co, PA
Census: 1870 in Chanceford, York Co, PA
Occupation: 1870 ; Keeping house[1, 77]
Probate: March 24, 1875 in Chanceford, York Co, PA[98]
Will: November 25, 1874 in Chanceford, York Co, PA[108]

Sarah "Sallie" Ann Gipe and Jacob Warner Oberlander had the
following children:

    i.   Luther Overlander (son of Jacob Warner Oberlander and
        Sarah "Sallie" Ann Gipe) was born in 1855 in PA.

    ii. Sarah Catherine Overlander (daughter of Jacob Warner
        Oberlander and Sarah "Sallie" Ann Gipe) was born in 1855
        in York Co, PA. She died in 1919. She married Casper
        Medwick. He was born in 1850.

    iii. Edward Overlander (son of Jacob Warner Oberlander and
        Sarah "Sallie" Ann Gipe) was born in 1857 in York Co, PA.

    iv. Adeline Overlander (daughter of Jacob Warner Oberlander
        and Sarah "Sallie" Ann Gipe) was born in 1858 in York Co,
        PA. She died in 1882. She married William Wright. He
        was born in 1850.

7.   v.   Rebecca Jane Overlander (daughter of Jacob Warner
        Oberlander and Sarah "Sallie" Ann Gipe) was born in
        October 1859 in Chanceford, York Co, PA[1, 28]. She died on
        November 20, 1921 in Hazleton State Hospital, Hazleton,
        Luzerne Co, PA[28, 66]. She married Joseph Pierce Layman
        (son of Michael Layman and Elmira Elizabeth Raymond) in
        1877 in Chanceford, York Co, PA[65]. He was born on
        January 08, 1859 in Airville, York Co, PA[1, 28, 32]. He died on

February 20, 1924 in Chicago, Cook Co, IL[62, 63, 64].

    vi. Caroline Overlander (daughter of Jacob Warner Oberlander and Sarah "Sallie" Ann Gipe) was born in 1861 in PA.

    vii. Samuel Washington Overlander (son of Jacob Warner Oberlander and Sarah "Sallie" Ann Gipe) was born in 1862 in York Co, PA. He died in 1945. He married Caroline "Carrie" Medwick. She was born in 1859 in PA.

    viii. Margaret "Maggie" Jane Overlander (daughter of Jacob Warner Oberlander and Sarah "Sallie" Ann Gipe) was born in 1864 in York Co, PA. She died in 1942. She married Charles Wesley Rexroth. He was born in 1859 in PA. He died in 1949.

    ix. Emaline Ellen Overlander (daughter of Jacob Warner Oberlander and Sarah "Sallie" Ann Gipe) was born in 1866 in York Co, PA. She died in 1949. She married Samuel David Rexroth. He was born in 1860.

    x. Barbara Alice Overlander (daughter of Jacob Warner Oberlander and Sarah "Sallie" Ann Gipe) was born in 1868 in York Co, PA. She married Tempest Valentine Myers.

    xi. Jacob L Overlander (son of Jacob Warner Oberlander and Sarah "Sallie" Ann Gipe) was born in 1869 in York Co, PA. He died in 1916. He married Sarah Amanda Heffner. She was born in 1871 in PA.

Generation 5

20. **John? McCloud** was born about Abt. 1780.

John? McCloud had the following child:

  10. i. David McCloud (son of John? McCloud) was born about Abt. 1807 in PA. He died before Bef. May 19, 1864 in Northumberland Co, PA[79]. He married Mary ? (daughter of ? and ?) about Abt. 1835 in Northumberland?, PA. She was born about Abt. 1815 in PA. She died between 1880-1900 in Northumberland Co, PA.

22. **?** was born in PA. He married **?**.

---

23.   **?** was born in PA.

   ? and ? had the following child:
   11.   i.   Mary ? (daughter of ? and ?) was born about Abt. 1815 in
               PA. She died between 1880-1900 in Northumberland Co,
               PA. She married David McCloud (son of John? McCloud)
               about Abt. 1835 in Northumberland?, PA. He was born
               about Abt. 1807 in PA. He died before Bef. May 19, 1864
               in Northumberland Co, PA[79].

24.   **Michael Layman** (son of Michael Layman and Rachel Neal) was born
      about Abt. 1795 in Milesburg, Northumberland (Centre) Co, PA[1]. He
      died about Abt. 1850 in Peach Bottom, York Co, PA[1]. He married
      Sarah Klein (daughter of Henry Kline and Catherine Surr) on June
      28, 1818 in Trinity Lutheran, New Holland, Lancaster Co, PA[1, 109, 110].

25.   **Sarah Klein** (daughter of Henry Kline and Catherine Surr) was born
      in 1796 in Manor, Lancaster Co, PA[1]. She died between 1850-1860 in
      Peach Bottom, York Co, PA[1, 111].

      More About Michael Layman:
      Census: 1800 in parents; w[112]
      Census: 1810 in Howard, Centre Co, PA[113]
      Census: 1820
      Census: 1830
      Census: 1840
      Census: 1850 in Peach Bottom, York Co, PA (Lyman)[91]
      Occupation: Abt. 1825 ; Farmer
      Occupation: Abt. 1830 ; Canal boatman[1]
      Occupation: 1850 ; Laborer[91]
      Religion: ; Methodist[1]

      Notes for Michael Layman:
      Died 1846, David R. Layman, Biography, source unknown.
      Cannot locate Michael in United States Census 1820-1840.

      More About Sarah Klein:
      Census: 1800 in parents; w
      Census: 1810 in parents; w
      Census: 1820 in Manor, Lancaster Co, PA[114]

Census: 1830 in husband; w
Census: 1840 in husband; w
Census: 1850 in Peach Bottom, York Co, PA
Religion: ; Lutheran[1]

Sarah Klein and Michael Layman had the following children:

12. i. Michael Layman (son of Michael Layman and Sarah Klein) was born on October 10, 1818 in Marietta, Lancaster Co, PA[1, 89]. He died on May 17, 1892 in Lower Chanceford, York Co, PA[1, 89]. He married Elmira Elizabeth Raymond (daughter of John Reiman and Nancy? ?) on April 03, 1845 in Christ Lutheran, Elizabethtown, Lancaster Co, PA[1]. She was born on January 17, 1824 in Maytown, York Co, PA[1]. She died on November 05, 1888 in Lower Chanceford, York Co, PA[1, 90].

ii. Catherine Layman (daughter of Michael Layman and Sarah Klein) was born about Abt. 1825 in PA.

iii. Christina Layman (daughter of Michael Layman and Sarah Klein) was born about Abt. 1825 in PA.

iv. Elizabeth Layman (daughter of Michael Layman and Sarah Klein) was born about Abt. 1825 in PA.

v. George Layman (son of Michael Layman and Sarah Klein) was born about Abt. 1825 in PA.

vi. Henry Layman (son of Michael Layman and Sarah Klein) was born in 1834 in PA. He married Isabelle ?. She was born in 1840.

vii. Sophia M Layman (daughter of Michael Layman and Sarah Klein) was born in 1834 in PA.

viii. David R Layman (son of Michael Layman and Sarah Klein) was born in 1841 in PA.

26. **John Reiman** was born about Abt. 1790 in Dauphin Co, PA. He died in 1841 in York Co, PA. He married **Nancy? ?** about Abt. 1820 in PA.

27. **Nancy? ?** was born about Abt. 1790 in PA. She died after Aft. 1841.

More About John Reiman:
Census: 1820 in West Manchester, York Co, PA[115]
Census: 1830 in York Co, PA
Census: 1840
Will: 1841 in York, York Co, PA[116]

Nancy? ? and John Reiman had the following child:

13.   i.   Elmira Elizabeth Raymond (daughter of John Reiman and
            Nancy? ?) was born on January 17, 1824 in Maytown,
            York Co, PA[1]. She died on November 05, 1888 in Lower
            Chanceford, York Co, PA[1, 90]. She married Michael
            Layman (son of Michael Layman and Sarah Klein) on April
            03, 1845 in Christ Lutheran, Elizabethtown, Lancaster Co,
            PA[1]. He was born on October 10, 1818 in Marietta,
            Lancaster Co, PA[1, 89]. He died on May 17, 1892 in Lower
            Chanceford, York Co, PA[1, 89].

28.   **Michael Baugher Oberlander** (son of Jacob Oberlander and Susan
       Baugher) was born on February 23, 1798 in Jefferson, Codorus, York
       Co, PA[96, 117, 118]. He died about Abt. 1880 in Chanceford, York Co,
       PA. He married **Maria Catherine Warner** (daughter of John Christian
       Warner and Maria Elizabeth Miller) on August 17, 1819 in First Trinity
       Reformed, Chanceford, York Co, PA[96].

29.   **Maria Catherine Warner** (daughter of John Christian Warner and
       Maria Elizabeth Miller) was born on March 21, 1798 in Hanover, York
       Co, PA[119, 120]. She died in 1848 in Chanceford, York Co, PA[96].

       More About Michael Baugher Oberlander:
       Baptism: May 09, 1798 in St. Matthews Lutheran, Hanover, York Co,
       PA[96]
       Burial: Abt. 1880 in Saint Lukes Evangelical Lutheran Cemetery, New
       Bridgeville, PA[121]
       Census: 1800 in father; Manheim, York Co, PA w[122]
       Census: 1810 in father; Shrewsburg, York Co, PA w[123]
       Census: 1820
       Census: 1830 in Upper Chanceford, York Co, PA[124]
       Census: 1840 in Chanceford, York Co, PA[125]
       Census: 1850 in Chanceford, York Co, PA[126]
       Census: 1860 in Chanceford, York Co, PA[102]
       Census: 1870 in Chanceford, York Co, PA[103]
       Census: 1880 in Chanceford, York Co, PA[127]

Naturalization:[128]
Occupation: 1850 ; Laborer
Occupation: 1860 ; Laborer[106]
Occupation: 1870 ; Shoemaker[103]
Occupation: 1880 ; Home[129]
Property: 1860 in $100[106]
Religion: ; Presbyterian[96]

More About Maria Catherine Warner:
Baptism: Bet. May 07-09 1798 in St. Jacobs (Stone) Union, Glenville, York Co, PA[120, 130]
Burial: 1848 in Saint Lukes Evangelical Lutheran Cemetery, New Bridgeville, PA[131]
Census: 1800 in father; Codorus, York Co, PA w[132]
Census: 1810 in father; Codorus, York Co, PA w[133]
Census: 1820 in husband; w
Census: 1830 in husband; Chanceford, York Co, PA w
Census: 1840 in husband; Chanceford, York Co, PA w

Notes for Maria Catherine Warner:
Baptism March 21, 1798, Warner family information, JWerner.txt, Don Varner, DRVarner@aol.com.

Maria Catherine Warner and Michael Baugher Oberlander had the following children:

     i. Catherine Oberlander (daughter of Michael Baugher Oberlander and Maria Catherine Warner) was born in PA.

     ii. Daniel Baugher Oberlander (son of Michael Baugher Oberlander and Maria Catherine Warner) was born in PA.

     iii. Peter Baugher Oberlander (son of Michael Baugher Oberlander and Maria Catherine Warner) was born in PA.

     iv. Samuel Oberlander (son of Michael Baugher Oberlander and Maria Catherine Warner) was born in PA.

     v. Sarah Ann Oberlander (daughter of Michael Baugher Oberlander and Maria Catherine Warner) was born in PA.

14.   vi. Jacob Warner Oberlander (son of Michael Baugher

Oberlander and Maria Catherine Warner) was born in 1819 in Chanceford, York Co, PA[1, 96]. He died on December 27, 1898 in Chanceford, York Co, PA[1, 96]. He married Sarah "Sallie" Ann Gipe (daughter of John Gipe and Elizabeth ?) on October 26, 1854 in St. Lukes (Stahleys) Lutheran, New Bridgeville, York Co, PA[1, 96, 97]. She was born in 1834 in Chanceford, York Co, PA[96]. She died on December 20, 1874 in Chanceford, York Co, PA[96, 98]. He married Catherine Margaret Gipe (daughter of John Gipe and Elizabeth ?) about Abt. 1845. She was born in 1826 in PA.

vii. Elizabeth Oberlander (daughter of Michael Baugher Oberlander and Maria Catherine Warner) was born in 1823 in PA. She married Jesse Runkle. He was born in 1821 in PA.

viii. Mary Jane Oberlander (daughter of Michael Baugher Oberlander and Maria Catherine Warner) was born in 1830 in York Co, PA. She married Peter Tome. He was born in 1825 in York Co, PA.

ix. Susan Warner Oberlander (daughter of Michael Baugher Oberlander and Maria Catherine Warner) was born in 1833 in PA.

x. William Oberlander (son of Michael Baugher Oberlander and Maria Catherine Warner) was born in 1833 in PA.

xi. Michael Baugher Oberlander (son of Michael Baugher Oberlander and Maria Catherine Warner) was born in 1835 in PA.

xii. Christian Oberlander (son of Michael Baugher Oberlander and Maria Catherine Warner) was born in 1838 in PA. He married Mary Dunlop?. She was born in 1846 in PA.

30. **John Gipe** (son of Jacob Gipe and Elizabeth ?) was born on October 17, 1790 in York Co, PA[134]. He died in 1845 in Chanceford, York Co, PA[134]. He married **Elizabeth ?** about Abt. 1815 in York Co, PA.

31. **Elizabeth ?** was born in 1795 in PA[134]. She died about Abt. 1861 in York Co, PA.

More About John Gipe:
Burial: 1845
Census: 1790 in father; York Co, PA w
Census: 1800 in parents; w
Census: 1810 in father; Chanceford, York Co, PA w[135]
Census: 1820 in Upper Chanceford, York Co, PA[136]
Census: 1830 in Upper Chanceford, York Co, PA (Giese)[137]
Census: 1840 in Chanceford, York Co, PA[138]

More About Elizabeth ?:
Census: 1800
Census: 1810
Census: 1820
Census: 1830 in husband; Upper Chanceford, York Co, PA w
Census: 1840 in husband; Chanceford, York Co, PA w[138]
Census: 1850 in South ward York, York Co, PA[139]
Census: 1860 in Jac. Oberlander); Chanceford, York Co, PA (Kipe w[102]

Elizabeth ? and John Gipe had the following children:

    i.   Elizabeth Gipe (daughter of John Gipe and Elizabeth ?) was born in PA.

    ii.   Mary "Polly" Gipe (daughter of John Gipe and Elizabeth ?) was born in 1824 in PA. She married John Smith. He was born in 1820.

    iii.   Catherine Margaret Gipe (daughter of John Gipe and Elizabeth ?) was born in 1826 in PA. She married Jacob Warner Oberlander (son of Michael Baugher Oberlander and Maria Catherine Warner) about Abt. 1845. He was born in 1819 in Chanceford, York Co, PA[1, 96]. He died on December 27, 1898 in Chanceford, York Co, PA[1, 96].

    More About Jacob Warner Oberlander:
    Burial: 1898
    Census: 1820 in parents; w
    Census: 1830 in father age 10; Upper Chanceford, York Co, PA w[99]
    Census: 1840 in father age 10; Upper Chanceford, York Co, PA w[100]

Census: 1850 in Chanceford, York Co, PA[101]
Census: 1860 in Chanceford, York Co, PA[1, 102]
Census: 1870 in Chanceford, York Co, PA[103]
Census: 1880 in Chanceford, York Co, PA[1, 104]
Occupation: Bet. 1850-1880 ; Farmer[77, 105, 106, 107]
Property: 1860 in $4000 + $640[106]
Property: 1870 in $4000 + $1500[77]
Religion: ; Lutheran[1]

iv. Michael Gipe (son of John Gipe and Elizabeth ?) was born in 1828 in PA.

v. Lena L Gipe (daughter of John Gipe and Elizabeth ?) was born about Abt. 1834 in PA.

15. vi. Sarah "Sallie" Ann Gipe (daughter of John Gipe and Elizabeth ?) was born in 1834 in Chanceford, York Co, PA[96]. She died on December 20, 1874 in Chanceford, York Co, PA[96, 98]. She married Jacob Warner Oberlander (son of Michael Baugher Oberlander and Maria Catherine Warner) on October 26, 1854 in St. Lukes (Stahleys) Lutheran, New Bridgeville, York Co, PA[1, 96, 97]. He was born in 1819 in Chanceford, York Co, PA[1, 96]. He died on December 27, 1898 in Chanceford, York Co, PA[1, 96].

vii. Amos Gipe (son of John Gipe and Elizabeth ?) was born in 1835 in PA.

viii. Lydia Gipe (daughter of John Gipe and Elizabeth ?) was born in 1837 in PA.

Generation 6

48. **Michael Layman** (son of John Jacob Loyman and Anna Margaret ?) was born on December 11, 1764 in Philadelphia, Philadelphia, PA[140, 141]. He died on January 05, 1843 in Howard, Centre Co, PA[1, 142]. He married **Rachel Neal** (daughter of Henry Neal) about Abt. 1794 in Northumberland?, PA.

49. **Rachel Neal** (daughter of Henry Neal) was born on December 04, 1765 in Buffalo Valley, Lancaster (Union) Co, PA[95]. She died on December 23, 1855 in Howard, Centre Co, PA[1, 143].

More About Michael Layman:

Baptism: January 12, 1765 in St. Michael's Zion Lutheran Church, Philadelphia, Philadelphia, PA[141]

Burial: 1843 in Howard Methodist Cemetery, Howard, Centre Co, PA[1, 142]

Census: 1790 in parents; w[144]

Census: 1800[145]

Census: 1810 in Howard, Centre Co, PA (Lyman)[146]

Census: 1820 in Howard, Centre Co, PA (Lyman)[147]

Census: 1830 in Howard, Centre Co, PA (Lymon)[148]

Census: 1840 in Howard, Centre Co, PA (Leyman)[149]

Military Service: Abt. 1780 ; American Revolution, Private 2nd PA Reg, ? Co, ? class (Philadelphia)[1, 95, 150, 151]

Occupation: Abt. 1790 ; Farmer[95, 140, 151]

Occupation: 1796 ; Carpenter[1, 152, 153]

Occupation: 1799 ; Joiner[154]

Occupation: 1810 ; Trade[155]

Occupation: 1820 ; Manufacturing[156]

Probate: Bet. May 10-June 08, 1843 in Centre Co, PA[157]

Religion: ; Methodist Episcopal[1, 140]

Residence: 1781 in Philadelphia, PA[158]

Residence: Bet. 1795-1803 in Northumberland (Union) Co, PA[95]

Residence: 1796 in West Buffalo, Northumberland (Union) Co, PA[159]

Residence: 1799 in Mifflinburg, Northumberland (Union) Co, PA[160]

Residence: 1806 in Mountain Eagle, Centre Co, PA[161]

Residence: 1810 in Centre, Centre Co, PA[155]

Will: January 02, 1843 in Howard Tp, Centre Co, PA[157, 162]

Notes for Michael Layman:

Michael was a member of a small group of soldiers that moved the Liberty Bell from Allentown to Philadelphia after Independence, Jack Lehman c/o Judy Spilsbury

Democrat, Michael Leyman, Commemorative Biographical Record, Northern PA.

Fought at Brandywine, PA

More About Rachel Neal:

Burial: 1855 in Howard Methodist Cemetery, Howard, Centre Co, PA[1, 143]

Census: 1790 in parents; w
Census: 1800
Census: 1810 in husband; Howard, Centre Co, PA w
Census: 1820 in husband; Howard, Centre Co, PA w
Census: 1830 in husband; Howard, Centre Co, PA w
Census: 1840 in husband; Howard, Centre Co, PA w
Census: 1850 in Howard, Centre Co, PA (son John Layman)[163]
Occupation: 1850 ; House & lot?[164]
Property: 1850 in $450[164]
Religion: ; Methodist[1]

Notes for Rachel Neal:
Born 1765 Duncan family information, Jack Lehman, North Charleston, SC

Rachel Neal and Michael Layman had the following children:
- i. Elizabeth Layman (daughter of Michael Layman and Rachel Neal) was born in PA.

- ii. Henry Layman (son of Michael Layman and Rachel Neal) was born in PA.

- iii. Jacob Layman (son of Michael Layman and Rachel Neal) was born in PA.

- iv. Rachel Layman (daughter of Michael Layman and Rachel Neal) was born in PA.

- v. Sarah Layman (daughter of Michael Layman and Rachel Neal) was born in PA.

24.   vi. Michael Layman (son of Michael Layman and Rachel Neal) was born about Abt. 1795 in Milesburg, Northumberland (Centre) Co, PA[1]. He died about Abt. 1850 in Peach Bottom, York Co, PA[1]. He married Sarah Klein (daughter of Henry Kline and Catherine Surr) on June 28, 1818 in Trinity Lutheran, New Holland, Lancaster Co, PA[1, 109, 110]. She was born in 1796 in Manor, Lancaster Co, PA[1]. She died between 1850-1860 in Peach Bottom, York Co, PA[1, 111].

vii. John Layman (son of Michael Layman and Rachel Neal) was born in 1812 in PA. He married Nancy ?. She was born in 1815 in Ireland (PA).

50. **Henry Kline** (son of Peter Michael? Klein and Anna Margaret? ?) was born about Abt. 1770 in Germany. He died in March 1832 in Safe Harbor, Conestoga, Lancaster Co, PA[165]. He married **Catherine Surr** about Abt. 1787 in Germany (PA).

51. **Catherine Surr** was born about Abt. 1770 in Germany. She died between 1810-1820 in Safe Harbor, Conestoga, Lancaster Co, PA[165].

More About Henry Kline:
Burial: 1832
Census: 1790
Census: 1800 in Manor, Lancaster Co, PA
Census: 1810 in Hempfield, Lancaster Co, PA[166]
Census: 1820 in West Hempfield, Lancaster Co, PA[167]
Census: 1830[168]
Immigration: Bef. 1796
Occupation: Abt. 1800 ; Cabinet maker[111]
Probate: June 18, 1832 in Lancaster Co, PA[169]
Residence: 1815 in Safe Harbor, Conestoga, Lancaster Co, PA[170]

Notes for Henry Kline:
Klein: German, Dutch (also de Klein(e)) from Middle High German, Dutch, German klein 'small', or Yiddish kleyn. This was a nickname for a person of small stature, but is also often found as a distinguishing name for a junior male, usually a son, in names such as Kleinhans and Kleinpeter. This name is common and widespread throughout central and eastern Europe.

More About Catherine Surr:
Census: 1790 in husband; w
Census: 1800 in husband; Lancaster Co, PA w
Census: 1810 in husband; Lancaster Co, PA w
Immigration: Bef. 1796

Catherine Surr and Henry Kline had the following children:

i. Christian Klein (son of Henry Kline and Catherine Surr) was born in 1788 in PA. He married Elizabeth ?. She was born in 1796 in PA.

ii. ? Klein (son of Henry Kline and Catherine Surr) was born about Abt. 1790.

iii. Elizabeth Klein (daughter of Henry Kline and Catherine Surr) was born about Abt. 1790.

iv. Peter Klein (son of Henry Kline and Catherine Surr) was born about Abt. 1790.

v. Susan Klein (daughter of Henry Kline and Catherine Surr) was born about Abt. 1790.

25.   vi. Sarah Klein (daughter of Henry Kline and Catherine Surr) was born in 1796 in Manor, Lancaster Co, PA[1]. She died between 1850-1860 in Peach Bottom, York Co, PA[1, 111]. She married Michael Layman (son of Michael Layman and Rachel Neal) on June 28, 1818 in Trinity Lutheran, New Holland, Lancaster Co, PA[1, 109, 110]. He was born about Abt. 1795 in Milesburg, Northumberland (Centre) Co, PA[1]. He died about Abt. 1850 in Peach Bottom, York Co, PA[1].

56. **Jacob Oberlander** (son of Peter Oberlander and Anna Maria Catherine Neipp) was born in 1768 in Berwick, York Co, PA[171]. He died on April 12, 1816 in Chanceford, York Co, PA[171, 172]. He married **Susan Baugher** (daughter of John George William Bager and Eva Catherine Kepner) in 1797 in Hanover, York Co, PA[173].

57. **Susan Baugher** (daughter of John George William Bager and Eva Catherine Kepner) was born in 1773 in Berwick, York Co, PA[172]. She died on April 21, 1814 in Chanceford, York Co, PA[172].

More About Jacob Oberlander:
Baptism: Abt. 1773 in St. Matthews Lutheran, Hanover, York Co, PA
Burial: 1816
Census: 1790 in parents; w
Census: 1800 in Manheim, York Co, PA (Overland)[174]
Census: 1810 in Shrewsburg, York Co, PA
Probate: Bet. May 14-December 18, 1816 in Chanceford, York Co,

Notes for Jacob Oberlander:
Jacob's children Peter & John were raised by brother Michael after father Jacob's death in 1816. Jacob's other minor children were given guardenship to Michael Miller, Probate files, 1816, Rep 39, York County Archives, York, PA, Deborah Hershey, Elizabethtown, PA, Dec 2008

Born what is now Montgomery Co, PA, Harry Diehl & Christie Fleming.
Moved to Chanceford, York Co, PA in 1811, Oberlander family information, p 30.

More About Susan Baugher:
Burial: 1814
Census: 1790 in father; York Co, PA w
Census: 1800 in husband; Manheim, York Co, PA w
Census: 1810 in husband; Shrewsburg, York Co, PA w

Susan Baugher and Jacob Oberlander had the following children:

28.   i.   Michael Baugher Oberlander (son of Jacob Oberlander and Susan Baugher) was born on February 23, 1798 in Jefferson, Codorus, York Co, PA[96, 117, 118]. He died about Abt. 1880 in Chanceford, York Co, PA. He married Maria Catherine Warner (daughter of John Christian Warner and Maria Elizabeth Miller) on August 17, 1819 in First Trinity Reformed, Chanceford, York Co, PA[96]. She was born on March 21, 1798 in Hanover, York Co, PA[119, 120]. She died in 1848 in Chanceford, York Co, PA[96]. He married Eva Warner (daughter of John Christian Warner and Maria Elizabeth Miller) about Abt. 1850. She was born in 1812 in PA.

      ii. Peter Oberlander (son of Jacob Oberlander and Susan Baugher) was born in 1799 in PA. He married Susan Fuhrman. She was born in 1802 in PA.

      iii. John Oberlander (son of Jacob Oberlander and Susan Baugher) was born in 1801 in PA.

iv. William Oberlander (son of Jacob Oberlander and Susan Baugher) was born in 1802 in PA.

v. Jacob Baugher Oberlander (son of Jacob Oberlander and Susan Baugher) was born in 1803 in PA. He died in 1887. He married Elizabeth Albright. She was born in 1810.

vi. Catherine Oberlander (daughter of Jacob Oberlander and Susan Baugher) was born in 1806 in PA.

vii. Elizabeth Oberlander (daughter of Jacob Oberlander and Susan Baugher) was born in 1807 in PA.

viii. Daniel Oberlander (son of Jacob Oberlander and Susan Baugher) was born in 1811 in PA. He married Leah ?. She was born in 1811 in PA.

ix. Samuel Oberlander (son of Jacob Oberlander and Susan Baugher) was born in 1812 in PA. He married Elizabeth ?. She was born in 1810 in PA.

x. Frederick Oberlander (son of Jacob Oberlander and Susan Baugher) was born in 1814 in PA.

58. **John Christian Warner** (son of John George Werner and Judith ?) was born on October 24, 1775 in York Co, PA[1, 119, 177, 178]. He died in 1842 in York Co, PA[119]. He married **Maria Elizabeth Miller** (daughter of Andrew Miller and Anna Maria Hamm) about Abt. 1797 in York Co, PA.

59. **Maria Elizabeth Miller** (daughter of Andrew Miller and Anna Maria Hamm) was born on October 17, 1777 in Cordorus, York Co, PA[1, 119, 179]. She died in 1848 in York Co, PA.

More About John Christian Warner:
Baptism: November 19, 1775 in St. Jacobs (Stone) Union, Glenville, York Co, PA[119, 177, 178, 180]
Burial: 1842
Census: 1790 in father; York Co, PA w
Census: 1800 in Codorus, York Co, PA
Census: 1810 in Codorus, York Co, PA[181]
Census: 1820 in Peach Bottom, York Co, PA[182]

Census: 1830 in Upper Chanceford, York Co, PA[183]
Census: 1840 in Chanceford, York Co, PA[184]
Will: June 22, 1842[185]

More About Maria Elizabeth Miller:
Baptism: 1779 in St. Jacobs (Stone) Union, Glenville, York Co, PA
Census: 1790 in father; Codorus, York Co, PA w
Census: 1800 in Cordorus, York Co, PA
Census: 1810 in Cordorus, York Co, PA
Census: 1820 in Peach Bottom, York Co, PA
Census: 1830 in Upper Chanceford, York Co, PA
Census: 1840 in Chanceford, York Co, PA
Census: 1850 in son Jacob; Chanceford, York Co, PA w[186]

Notes for Maria Elizabeth Miller:
Most show Maria as daughte rof Anna Maria Hamm (ages 13 when born), but could'v ebeen daughte rof other wife, Anna Cath. Grokes [author, 2007]

Maria Elizabeth Miller and John Christian Warner had the following children:

29.   i.   Maria Catherine Warner (daughter of John Christian Warner and Maria Elizabeth Miller) was born on March 21, 1798 in Hanover, York Co, PA[119, 120]. She died in 1848 in Chanceford, York Co, PA[96]. She married Michael Baugher Oberlander (son of Jacob Oberlander and Susan Baugher) on August 17, 1819 in First Trinity Reformed, Chanceford, York Co, PA[96]. He was born on February 23, 1798 in Jefferson, Codorus, York Co, PA[96, 117, 118]. He died about Abt. 1880 in Chanceford, York Co, PA.

   ii.   Samuel Warner (son of John Christian Warner and Maria Elizabeth Miller) was born in 1800 in PA. He died in 1839. He married Catherine Bowman. She was born in 1810.

   iii.   Jacob Warner (son of John Christian Warner and Maria Elizabeth Miller) was born in 1803 in PA. He married Catherine ?. She was born in 1808 in PA.

   iv.   Elizabeth Warner (daughter of John Christian Warner and Maria Elizabeth Miller) was born in 1805 in PA. She died in

1842. She married John Wise. He was born in 1800.

v. Henry Warner (son of John Christian Warner and Maria Elizabeth Miller) was born in 1805 in PA.

vi. Eva Warner (daughter of John Christian Warner and Maria Elizabeth Miller) was born in 1812 in PA. She married Michael Baugher Oberlander (son of Jacob Oberlander and Susan Baugher) about Abt. 1850. He was born on February 23, 1798 in Jefferson, Codorus, York Co, PA[96, 117, 118]. He died about Abt. 1880 in Chanceford, York Co, PA.

More About Eva Warner:
b: 1812

More About Michael Baugher Oberlander:
Baptism: May 09, 1798 in St. Matthews Lutheran, Hanover, York Co, PA[96]
Burial: Abt. 1880 in Saint Lukes Evangelical Lutheran Cemetery, New Bridgeville, PA[121]
Census: 1800 in father; Manheim, York Co, PA w[122]
Census: 1810 in father; Shrewsburg, York Co, PA w[123]
Census: 1820
Census: 1830 in Upper Chanceford, York Co, PA[124]
Census: 1840 in Chanceford, York Co, PA[125]
Census: 1850 in Chanceford, York Co, PA[126]
Census: 1860 in Chanceford, York Co, PA[102]
Census: 1870 in Chanceford, York Co, PA[103]
Census: 1880 in Chanceford, York Co, PA[127]
Naturalization:[128]
Occupation: 1850 ; Laborer
Occupation: 1860 ; Laborer[106]
Occupation: 1870 ; Shoemaker[103]
Occupation: 1880 ; Home[129]
Property: 1860 in $100[106]
Religion: ; Presbyterian[96]

vii. John Warner (son of John Christian Warner and Maria Elizabeth Miller) was born in 1815 in PA. He died in 1869. He married Elizabeth Workinger. She was born in 1814 in PA.

viii. Samuel Warner (son of John Christian Warner and Maria Elizabeth Miller) was born in 1815 in PA. He married Elizabeth ?. She was born in 1816 in PA.

60. **Jacob Gipe** (son of John Nicholas Geib and Anna Charlotte Dietz) was born about Abt. 1761 in York Co, PA[134]. He died on December 18, 1843 in Chanceford, York Co, PA[134, 187]. He married **Elizabeth ?** about Abt. 1782 in York Co, PA.

61. **Elizabeth ?** was born about Abt. 1762[134]. She died between 1810-1820 in York Co, PA[134].

More About Jacob Gipe:
Burial: 1843
Census: 1790 in York Co, PA
Census: 1800
Census: 1810 in Chanceford, York Co, PA[135]
Census: 1820 in Upper Chanceford, York Co, PA[136]
Census: 1830 in Upper Chanceford, York Co, PA (Geise)[188]
Census: 1840 in Chanceford, York Co, PA[189]
Occupation: Abt. 1800 ; Farmer[134]
Probate: Bet. April 04, 1844-December 18, 1845 in Chanceford, York Co, PA[190, 191]
Religion: ; St. Lukes (Stahleys) Lutheran, New Bridgeville, York Co, PA[134]
Residence: 1783 in Windsor, York Co, PA[192]

More About Elizabeth ?:
Census: 1790 in husband; York Co, PA w
Census: 1800 in husband; w
Census: 1810 in husband; Chanceford, York Co, PA w

Elizabeth ? and Jacob Gipe had the following children:
    i. Catherine Gipe (daughter of Jacob Gipe and Elizabeth ?) was born in 1785 in PA. She died in 1852. She married Adam Strayer. He was born in 1794 in PA.

ii.   Anna Margaret "Peggy" Gipe (daughter of Jacob Gipe and Elizabeth ?) was born in 1787 in PA. She died about Abt. 1825. She married Frederick Baymiller. He was born about Abt. 1780.

30.   iii.   John Gipe (son of Jacob Gipe and Elizabeth ?) was born on October 17, 1790 in York Co, PA[134]. He died in 1845 in Chanceford, York Co, PA[134]. He married Elizabeth ? about Abt. 1815 in York Co, PA. She was born in 1795 in PA[134]. She died about Abt. 1861 in York Co, PA.

iv.   Jacob Gipe (son of Jacob Gipe and Elizabeth ?) was born in 1793 in PA.

v.   Maria Magdalena "Polly" Gipe (daughter of Jacob Gipe and Elizabeth ?) was born in 1795 in PA. She died about Abt. 1830. She married John Hivner. He was born about Abt. 1790.

vi.   Daniel Gipe (son of Jacob Gipe and Elizabeth ?) was born about Abt. 1797 in PA.

vii.   Lydia Gipe (daughter of Jacob Gipe and Elizabeth ?) was born in 1801 in PA.

Generation 7

96.   **John Jacob Loyman** was born about Abt. 1740 in Germany. He died after Aft. February 06, 1785 in Lancaster Co, PA. He married **Anna Margaret ?** about Abt. 1760 in Germany.

97.   **Anna Margaret ?** was born about Abt. 1740 in Germany. She died in 1786 in Lancaster Co, PA[95].

More About John Jacob Loyman:
Burial: 1785
Immigration: Abt. 1764 ; Germany to USA[193]
Residence: Bet. 1764-1765 in Philadelphia, PA[194]
Will: February 06, 1785 in Conestoga Tp, Lancaster Co, PA[195]

Notes for John Jacob Loyman:
American Revolution, 5th-8th class, 8th Co (Philadelphia, PA, age

may restrict service)

Layman, Lehman, Lehmann:Americanized spelling of German Lehmann. German: variant of Lay 3. German: see Lehmann. German: status name for a feudal tenant or vassal, Middle High German leheman, lenman (from lehen 'to hold land as a feudal tenant' + man 'man'). The tenant held land on loan for the duration of his life in return for rent or service, but was not free to transfer or divide it.

More About Anna Margaret ?:
Immigration: Abt. 1764 ; Germany to USA (w/husband)
Probate: 1786 in Lancaster Co, PA[196]

Anna Margaret ? and John Jacob Loyman had the following children:

 i. Abraham Layman (son of John Jacob Loyman and Anna Margaret ?).

 ii. Daniel Layman (son of John Jacob Loyman and Anna Margaret ?).

 iii. Elizabeth Layman (daughter of John Jacob Loyman and Anna Margaret ?).

 iv. Henry Layman (son of John Jacob Loyman and Anna Margaret ?).

 v. Jacob Layman (son of John Jacob Loyman and Anna Margaret ?).

 vi. John Layman (son of John Jacob Loyman and Anna Margaret ?).

48. vii. Michael Layman (son of John Jacob Loyman and Anna Margaret ?) was born on December 11, 1764 in Philadelphia, Philadelphia, PA[140, 141]. He died on January 05, 1843 in Howard, Centre Co, PA[1, 142]. He married Rachel Neal (daughter of Henry Neal) about Abt. 1794 in Northumberland?, PA. She was born on December 04, 1765 in Buffalo Valley, Lancaster (Union) Co, PA[95]. She died on December 23, 1855 in Howard, Centre Co, PA[1, 143].

98. **Henry Neal** was born about Abt. 1740 in Buffalo Valley, Lancaster (Union) Co, PA. He died after Aft. 1809 in Northumberland (Union) Co, PA. He married an unknown spouse about Abt. 1770 in Northumberland (Union) Co, PA.

Henry Neal had the following children:

49. i. Rachel Neal (daughter of Henry Neal) was born on December 04, 1765 in Buffalo Valley, Lancaster (Union) Co, PA[95]. She died on December 23, 1855 in Howard, Centre Co, PA[1, 143]. She married Michael Layman (son of John Jacob Loyman and Anna Margaret ?) about Abt. 1794 in Northumberland?, PA. He was born on December 11, 1764 in Philadelphia, Philadelphia, PA[140, 141]. He died on January 05, 1843 in Howard, Centre Co, PA[1, 142].

ii. ? Neal (son of Henry Neal).

iii. ? Neal (daughter of Henry Neal).

100. **Peter Michael? Klein** was born about Abt. 1740. He died in March 1806 in Manor Tp, Lancaster Co, PA[197, 198]. He married **Anna Margaret? ?** about Abt. 1765.

101. **Anna Margaret? ?** was born about Abt. 1740. She died after Aft. 1775 in PA.

More About Peter Michael? Klein:
Burial: 1806
Probate: March 26, 1806 in Manor Tp, Lancaster Co, PA
Will: March 10, 1806 in Manor Tp, Lancaster Co, PA

Anna Margaret? ? and Peter Michael? Klein had the following children:

i. Peter? Kline (son of Peter Michael? Klein and Anna Margaret? ?) was born about Abt. 1768.

50. ii. Henry Kline (son of Peter Michael? Klein and Anna Margaret? ?) was born about Abt. 1770 in Germany. He died in March 1832 in Safe Harbor, Conestoga, Lancaster Co, PA[165]. He married Catherine Surr about Abt. 1787 in Germany (PA). She was born about Abt. 1770 in Germany. She died between 1810-1820 in Safe Harbor, Conestoga, Lancaster Co, PA[165].

iii. Jacob? Kline (son of Peter Michael? Klein and Anna
      Margaret? ?) was born about Abt. 1772.

iv.   Christopher? Kline (son of Peter Michael? Klein and Anna
      Margaret? ?) was born about Abt. 1774.

112. **Peter Oberlander** was born on January 01, 1745 in Germany. He
     died on December 28, 1780 in Heidelberg, Lancaster (Lebanon) Co,
     PA[171, 172, 199]. He married **Anna Maria Catherine Neipp** about Abt.
     1765 in Germany (PA).

113. **Anna Maria Catherine Neipp** was born in 1749 in Germany. She
     died on April 01, 1777 in Lancaster Co, PA.

More About Peter Oberlander:
Burial: 1780
Immigration: 1766[200]
Probate: December 28, 1780 in Heidelberg, Lancaster Co, PA[199]
Religion: 1776 ; Heidelberg Church, Schaffertown, Lebanon Co, PA[201]
Residence: 1766 in Philadelphia, PA[202]
Will: May 01, 1777 in Heidelberg, Lancaster Co, PA[199]

Notes for Peter Oberlander:
Births generally recorded at Jan 1 are estimate

Died 1777 Shafferstown, Berks Co, PA Christie Fleming,
CFleming@eagle.org & source unknown

Oberlander, Overlander: German (Oberländer) topographic or
habitational name from Oberland, meaning 'higher land', especially in
the Alps, where it refers to a settled plateau above the valley bottom.

More About Anna Maria Catherine Neipp:
Burial: 1777
Immigration: Abt. 1760

Notes for Anna Maria Catherine Neipp:

Neipp: Belgium and the Coat of Arms contains Blue shield a chevron between two gold roses and a acorn in base. Spelling variations include: Neipp, Neipe, Neippe, Niepee, Neipee, Neippee and others. First found in Belgium, where the name became noted for its many branches in the region, each house acquiring a status and influence which was envied by the princes of the region. Some of the first settlers of this name or some of its variants were: Many settlers were recorded from the mid 17th century onward in the great migration from Europe to the New World.

Also Anna Elizabeth

Anna Maria Catherine Neipp and Peter Oberlander had the following child:

56.   i.   Jacob Oberlander (son of Peter Oberlander and Anna Maria Catherine Neipp) was born in 1768 in Berwick, York Co, PA[171]. He died on April 12, 1816 in Chanceford, York Co, PA[171, 172]. He married Susan Baugher (daughter of John George William Bager and Eva Catherine Kepner) in 1797 in Hanover, York Co, PA[173]. She was born in 1773 in Berwick, York Co, PA[172]. She died on April 21, 1814 in Chanceford, York Co, PA[172].

114. **John George William Bager** was born on April 15, 1750 in Simmern, Rhineland-Palatinate, Germany[203, 204, 205]. He died on May 17, 1798 in Berwick, York Co, PA. He married **Eva Catherine Kepner** about Abt. 1770 in York?, PA.

115. **Eva Catherine Kepner** was born on June 09, 1753 in Germany. She died on March 11, 1803 in Berwick, York Co, PA[203].

More About John George William Bager:
Burial: 1798
Census: 1790 in York Co, PA[206]
Immigration: October 23, 1752 ; Germany to USA (ship Bawley, w/father)[207]
Residence: Bet. 1775-1788 in Berwick, York Co, PA[208, 209, 210]
Will: May 17, 1798 in Berwick, York Co, PA[204, 211, 212]

Notes for John George William Bager:
s/o John George Baugher b1725 Winnweiler, Rhineland-Palatinate,

Germany & Anna Elizabeth Schwab of Geissen, Hesse, Germany
s/o John George Bager b1680 Wiesbaum, Flonhein, Rhineland-Palatinate, Germany & Amelia Dorothy Elizabeth Lotz
d/o John Joseph Schwab b1697 Germany & Anna Barbara Rocker
s/o John Jacob Bager b1650 Saarland, Germany & Anna Elizabeth Jess
d/o John Henry Lotz b1642 Germany & Maria Catherine Rocker
s/o John Martin Schwab
d/o John Rocker & Anna ?
s/o George Bager b1620 Saarland, Germany
d/o Daniel Jess bc1620 Weisbaden, Hesse, Germany
d/o Burkhart Luzius Lotz b1613 Flonheim, Rhineland-Palatinate, Germany & Catherine Weinrich
s/o Philip Hartman Rocker b1640 Germany & Maria Imhoff?
d/o Casper Weinrich

Father's house is PA Historic Places, John George Bager Home, Abbottstown, Adams Co, PA, Dorothy Dillon, 6000 Lake Shore Dr., Evansville, IN 47712.

Bager Homestead (John George), Abbotstown, Adams, PA

Baugher: Americanized spelling of German Bager or Bäger (see Beger), or Bacher.

REVEREND JOHN GEORGE BAUGHER
The first mention of the Bagers in Wiesbaden, Germany was in 1658 when Rev. Bager's grandmother, the widow of Georg Bager, was named. Two sons are named: Hans Jacob Bager, father of the pastor, and his brother, Georg Leonhard Bager (1664-1687), a bricklayer. Both sons married Lutheran women and their children were baptized in their mother's faith, which was also the faith of the reigning class. Georg Leonhard Bager in 1684 was the father of three sons and one daughter. Hans Jacob had two sons in 1684, and by 1690 he had three sons. The maiden name of the mother, Jess (also Jesche and Jessge) was not familiar in Weisbaden and is first mentioned in 1651 as Leutant Daniel Jess in 1654 and 1663. He could be the father of Anna Elizabeth Jess who married Hans Jacob Bager. At age seventy, John George Bager took his Catholic father to live with him and he converted to the Lutheran church. This act was worthy of entry by the Pastor Hildebrand into the church records. The Reverend John George Bager I was born December 30, 1680 in

Wiesbaden, Germany, the son of Hans (John) Jacob Bager, Catholic, and Anna Elizabeth Jess, Evangelical (Lutheran), who were bakers by trade. This son was baptized on January 2, 1681 in Wiesbaden. John Georg Bager was taught reading, writing, catechism, arithmetic and music by Kantar Cruetzer; and Rectar Wagner taught him Latin. At age fourteen Bager went to Gymnasium (German high school). He received higher education in grammar, logic, rhetoric, Greek, religion and mathematics. On July 26, 1702 Bager matriculated at Jena. For two and one-fourth years he studied Hebrew under Magister Rupus and Theology under D. Hebenstreit. After five semesters he left Jena and registered in Strasburg. With help from Dr. W. Rohrbach, Bager gained a clear understanding of his education. He did not become a moderator in a Latin school or a school teacher in a church parish-he became a tutor to the Lutheran pastor in Freimershein; then to an official Stutz and pastor Lotz in Flonheim, Rheingrabskalt Dhaur. The acquaintance with these two people led to advancement, and both were also government officials. Pastor Lotz became his father-in-law when on December 4, 1708, the year of his pastoral assignment, John Georg Bager married Amalie Dorothea Elisabeth Lotz, the oldest daughter of the Flonheim pastor, Johann Helferich Lotz and his second wife, Maria Katharina Rocker.

Heinrich Lotz was born in Wehrda in 1570 and on January 23, 1595 he was hired as a cabinetmaker and miller in Marburg, Germany. On March 8, 1608 he was put in charge of the clock and water department. Heinrich's son, Pastor Burkhard Lotze (Lusius) was born in Marburg on June 13, 1613. He studied Theology in Marburg and Strasburg, and on October 5, 1641 he was married in Marburg to Katharine Weinreich, the daughter of Caspar Weinreich who died in Herstein. Pastor Burkhard Lotze died in Flonheim on November 11, 1676 and left his son, Johann Helferich Lotz to serve as pastor. The wife of Burkhard Lotze died on February 3, 1682.

Johann Helferich Lotz was born on November 17, 1642 in Wachterlisbach, the son of Pastor Burkhard Lotze. He studied Theology and became the pastor in Katherinenburg in Lower Alsace, where he married as his first wife the widow of his predecesso, Andreas Schmid. Her maiden name was Anna Sara Barth. This couple served this pastorage from April 13, 1675 through the invasion of the troops of Ludwig XIV and were forced to flee to Alsace, staying in exile from 1675 until 1676 in Frankfort. In 1676, Rev. Bager took the first pastorate in Flonheim where his first wife died on February 24, 1687, leaving him with six children.

As his second wife, Rev. Lotz married Maria Katharine Rocker, the daughter of a fellow pastor, Phillip Hartmann Rocker, in Barnheim and they were the parents of Amalie Lotz who married John Georg Bager. Reverend Bager took over the pastorate in Bernheim, and in 1712 he left this pastorate and accepted the call of Count Friedrich Ludwig von Nassau-Ottweiler to come to Niederlinxweiler.

Reverend John Georg Bager I and Amalie Lotz had twelve children-seven sons and five daughters. Two sons died at birth, one died in infancy, and one at about twenty-four years of age. One son left home at an early age and his fate is unknown. On April 4, 1735, Amalie died at age forty-six. The youngest child was four years of age. Amalie's mother, Maria Katharina Rocker Lotz, a widow since 1711, moved to Niederlinxweiler and cared for the orphaned family. She died February 7, 1746. Male descendants are known from only one son, Rev. John George Bager (Baugher) II, who came to America, landing in Philadelphia on October 23, 1752 on the ship Rawley. The same day he took his vows on allegiance to America. After serving as a pastor for over fifty years, Rev. John Georg Bager I died in 1764. The household inventory after his death showed a home well furnished for a good living, with pine furniture, utensils of copper, brass and pewter and plenty of table and bed linens. There was also a library of forty volumes, mainly on Theology. Each of the five living heirs received four or five books, but the son in America received only the Weimarische Bible, which was believed to be of high value. At that time Johann Georg Bager I had fifty-two grandchildren of which six were married, and twelve great-grandchildren.

Source: From a German translation of the ancestry of Reverend John Georg Bager/Baugher II of Germany   and Pennsylvania, Courtesy: Madaline Baugher of Weatherford, OK (received by Barbara Russell of California ca 1982)

Johannes Georgius Bager II (Rev. John George Baugher) was born on March 29, 1725 at Niederlinxweiler near Ottweiler in Nassau Saarbrücken, Germany. He became pastor of the Lutheran congregation of St. David's (Sherman's) Church on December 16, 1752 and moved to Hanover, PA on March 10, 1753. Rev. Bager's wife, Elisabetha Schwab (Swope) was born December 4, 1728 at Giessen in Hessen Darmstadt, Germany and their children were:

  I. John Georg Wilhelm (William) Bager, born at Simmern, Germany on April 15, 1750 (ancestor of your writer)

  II. Carl Theodor Frederick Bager born in 1751 at Simmern died and was buried at Helvertstuys, Holland.

III. Catharine Margaretha Bager was born January 9, 1753 at Quitopsen Hill in Lebanon Township, Lancaster County
and was baptized January 21, 1753.

IV. Christian Frederick Bager was born August 19, 1754 at Canawacken, Heidelberg Township, York County and was
baptized September 11, 1754.

V. Daniel Bager was born March 30, 1756 in Heidelberg Township and baptized April 6, 1756.

VI. Anna Maria Bager was born October 20, 1757 and baptized November 1, 1757.

VII. John Georg Bager was born April 9, 1759, baptized April 26 and died June 12, 1759.

VIII. John Jacob Bager was born November 5, 1760 in Conewago Township and baptized December 14, 1760.

IX. John Nicolaus Bager was born November 10, 1762 in Berwick Township and baptized December 5, 1762.

Dieter Cunz in The Maryland Germans states that in Baltimore "In the year 1756 or 1757, the congregation (of the German Lutheran Church) purchased a lot on which to erect a church... From a report probably written by Charles Frederick Wiesenthal, we learn that the 'first regularly officiating pastor' was the Reverend Georg Bager. A native of Simmern in the Hunstruck, Germany, he had come to America in 1752, and had held the laborious office of preacher for all the far-flung Lutherans in the Pennsylvania counties of York, Adams, Cumberland and Franklin. The Lutherans of Baltimore pleaded with him to include them in his circuit, and in 1755 he finally yielded to their request. For three consecutive years Rev. Bager came down from Pennsylvania six times a year, administering the spiritual functions in preaching and sacraments, and enjoying from this not more than five pounds a year. This was next to nothing indeed, as a reward, however, consisting only of eleven persons and the majority of them having no superfluous means, the good man was satisfied with it until the journey of over sixty miles became too arduous for him and he accepted another call."

During the fourth generation of the Runkles in York County, Jesse Runkle (1821-1894) married a descendant of Rev. Baugher's oldest son, William Baugher. Another descendant of Rev. Baugher married Christian Tome and was the mother of Jacob Tome, financier of Chanceford Township. Sam Saylor, who started this Runkle research, is descended from Christian Tome.

Reverend Baugher delivered his Valedictory sermon on May 1, 1763. The text was: Philippians 1: 27 and 28: "But whatever happens to me, remember always to live as Christians should, so that, whether I ever see you again or not, I will keep on hearing good reports that you are standing side by side with one strong purpose-to tell the Good News fearlessly, no matter what your enemies may do. They will see this as a sign of their downfall, but for you it will be a clear sign from God that he is with you, and that he has given you eternal life with him." Source: The Living Biblle

Rev. John George Baugher died in 1791 at age 66 and a marble stone marks his burial spot in St. John's Lutheran Cemetery in Abbottstown, PA. The stone says: "They were lovely in their lives, and in death they were not parted."

A grandson of Rev. Baugher, Rev. Henry Louis Baugher, was born July 18, 1800 at Abbottstown, Adams County, PA, the son of Christian Frederick and Ann Catharine Baugher. Reverend Dr. H. L. Baugher gave the benediction after President Abraham Lincoln spoke his famous Gettysburg Address, and later became the President of Gettysburg College. H. L. Baugher died on April 14, 1868. This was the program for the activities at the dedication of the Gettysburg Cemetery:

Music, by BIRGFIELD'S Band.

Prayer, by REV. T. H. STOCKTON, D.D.

Music, by the MARINE BAND.

Oration, by Hon. EDWARD EVERETT

Hymn composed by B. B. FRENCH, Esq., sung by Choir selected for the occasion.

Dedicatory Remarks, by the PRESIDENT OF THE UNITED STATES.

Benediction, by REV. H. L. BAUGHER, D.D.

More About Eva Catherine Kepner:
Census: 1790 in husband; York Co, PA w
Immigration: Bef. 1773

Notes for Eva Catherine Kepner:
aka Meads?

Eva Catherine Kepner and John George William Bager had the following children:

57.   i.   Susan Baugher (daughter of John George William Bager and Eva Catherine Kepner) was born in 1773 in Berwick,

York Co, PA[172]. She died on April 21, 1814 in Chanceford, York Co, PA[172]. She married Jacob Oberlander (son of Peter Oberlander and Anna Maria Catherine Neipp) in 1797 in Hanover, York Co, PA[173]. He was born in 1768 in Berwick, York Co, PA[171]. He died on April 12, 1816 in Chanceford, York Co, PA[171, 172].

ii.   Elizabeth Baugher (daughter of John George William Bager and Eva Catherine Kepner) was born in 1775 in York (Adams) Co, PA. She married Jacob Regal.

iii. Barbara Baugher (daughter of John George William Bager and Eva Catherine Kepner) was born about Abt. 1780 in PA. She married James Dustin.

iv.   Catherine Baugher (daughter of John George William Bager and Eva Catherine Kepner) was born about Abt. 1780 in PA. She married Solomon Hahn.

v.   Mary Baugher (daughter of John George William Bager and Eva Catherine Kepner) was born about Abt. 1780 in PA.

vi.   William Baugher (son of John George William Bager and Eva Catherine Kepner) was born in 1784 in York (Adams) Co, PA.

vii. Christina Baugher (daughter of John George William Bager and Eva Catherine Kepner) was born in 1786 in York (Adams) Co, PA.

viii. Anna Baugher (daughter of John George William Bager and Eva Catherine Kepner) was born in 1788 in PA.

116. **John George Werner** was born on February 23, 1754 in PA[119]. He died on August 16, 1805 in Codorus, York Co, PA[119]. He married **Judith ?** about Abt. 1770 in York?, PA.

117. **Judith ?** was born in March 1746[119]. She died on January 12, 1829 in Codorus, York Co, PA[119].

More About John George Werner:

Burial: 1805 in St. Jacobs (Stone) Union, Glenville, York Co, PA[179]
Census: 1790 in York Co, PA[213]
Census: 1800 in Manheim, York Co, PA
Immigration: Abt. 1755 ; Germany to USA (ship Brother)[119]
Probate: August 16, 1805 in Codorus, York Co, PA[214]
Will: July 10, 1805 in Codorus, York Co, PA[214, 215]

Notes for John George Werner:
s/o Joseph Varner of Bavaria, Germany

s/o John Adam Werner b1708 Masenbach, B-W, Germany &
Catherine Weber

More About Judith ?:
Burial: 1829
Census: 1790 in York Co, PA
Census: 1800 in Manheim, York Co, PA
Census: 1810
Census: 1820

Judith ? and John George Werner had the following children:

    i.   John Warner (son of John George Werner and Judith ?) was born in 1771 in PA.

    ii.   Charles "Carl" Warner (son of John George Werner and Judith ?) was born about Abt. 1772 in PA.

    iii.   Henry Warner (son of John George Werner and Judith ?) was born about Abt. 1772 in PA.

58.   iv.   John Christian Warner (son of John George Werner and Judith ?) was born on October 24, 1775 in York Co, PA[1, 119, 177, 178]. He died in 1842 in York Co, PA[119]. He married Maria Elizabeth Miller (daughter of Andrew Miller and Anna Maria Hamm) about Abt. 1797 in York Co, PA. She was born on October 17, 1777 in Cordorus, York Co, PA[1, 119, 179]. She died in 1848 in York Co, PA.

    v.   Catherine Warner (daughter of John George Werner and Judith ?) was born in 1778 in PA.

vi. Jacob Warner (son of John George Werner and Judith ?) was born in 1782 in PA. He died about Abt. 1785.

vii. Elizabeth Warner (daughter of John George Werner and Judith ?) was born in 1784 in PA.

viii. Jacob Warner (son of John George Werner and Judith ?) was born in 1786 in PA. He married Julia Cramer. She was born about Abt. 1790. He married Catherine Elizabeth Cramer. She was born about Abt. 1790.

ix. Anna Maria Warner (daughter of John George Werner and Judith ?) was born in 1790 in PA.

x. Maria Catherine Warner (daughter of John George Werner and Judith ?) was born in 1791 in PA.

118. **Andrew Miller** was born on March 14, 1752 in York Co, PA[179, 216]. He died on November 22, 1842 in Codorus, York Co, PA[179, 217, 218, 219]. He married **Anna Maria Hamm** about Abt. 1777 in York Co, PA.

119. **Anna Maria Hamm** was born on November 10, 1763 in York Co, PA[220]. She died on June 22, 1797 in York Co, PA[218, 221].

More About Andrew Miller:
Burial: 1842 in Emanuels (Jefferson) Union Cemetery, Jefferson, York Co, PA[179]
Census: 1790 in Codorus, York Co, PA[222]
Census: 1800 in Codorus, York Co, PA (Meller)
Census: 1810 in Codorus, York Co, PA[223]
Census: 1820 in Codorus, York Co, PA[224]
Census: 1830 in Codorus, York Co, PA[225]
Census: 1840 in Codorus, York Co, PA[226]
Census: 1841 in Old Codorus, York Co, PA[227]
Military Service: Abt. 1780 ; American Revolution, Private PA Reg (York)[228]
Occupation: ; Camp Security (York)[229]
Probate: December 14, 1842 in Codorus, York Co, PA[230]
Will: May 11, 1829 in Codorus, York Co, PA[230]

Notes for Andrew Miller:

s/o George Mueller 1720 B-W, Germany & Mary Barbara Stambach Bas-Rhine, France
s/o Andreas Miller b1716 Germany & Barbara Noll/Renoll
d/o Johannes Stambach c1676 Kutzenhausen, Alsace, France & Maria Catherine Meyer c 1690 Merzweiler, Alsace, France
s/o Michael Miller b1690 Germany & Christine ?
s/o Felix Stambach 1643 Alsace, France & Anna Maria Wehrling c1656
d/o Jacob Meyer b1653 Merzweiler, Alsace, France & Anna ?
s/o Ulrich Stambach b1620 Alsace, France

Miller: English and Scottish: occupational name for a miller. The standard modern vocabulary word represents the northern Middle English term, an agent derivative of mille 'mill', reinforced by Old Norse mylnari (see Milner). In southern, western, and central England Millward (literally, 'mill keeper') was the usual term. The American surname has absorbed many cognate surnames from other European languages, for example French Meunier, Dumoulin, Demoulins, and Moulin; German Mueller; Dutch Molenaar; Italian Molinaro; Spanish Molinero; Hungarian Molnár; Slavic Mlinar, etc.

More About Anna Maria Hamm:
Baptism: January 01, 1764 in York Co, PA[231]
Burial: 1797
Census: 1790 in Codorus, York Co, PA w/husband

Notes for Anna Maria Hamm:
d/o Daniel Ham b c1738 Germany & Barbara ? b1726

Hamm: English: topographic name from Old English hamm, denoting a patch of flat, low-lying alluvial land beside a stream (often a promontory or water meadow in a river bend), or a habitational name from any of numerous places named with this word, for example in Gloucestershire, Greater London, Kent, Somerset, and Wiltshire. German: topographic name for someone who lived on land in a river bend, Old High German ham (see 1 above). German habitational name from Hamm, a city in Westphalia.

Anna Maria Hamm and Andrew Miller had the following children:

59. i.   Maria Elizabeth Miller (daughter of Andrew Miller and Anna Maria Hamm) was born on October 17, 1777 in Cordorus, York Co, PA[1, 119, 179]. She died in 1848 in York Co, PA. She married John Christian Warner (son of John George Werner and Judith ?) about Abt. 1797 in York Co, PA. He was born on October 24, 1775 in York Co, PA[1, 119, 177, 178]. He died in 1842 in York Co, PA[119].

     ii. Catherine Miller (daughter of Andrew Miller and Anna Maria Hamm) was born in 1779 in York Co, PA.

     iii. Margaret Miller (daughter of Andrew Miller and Anna Maria Hamm) was born in 1782 in York Co, PA. She married John Gorrence.

     iv. Anna Christina Miller (daughter of Andrew Miller and Anna Maria Hamm) was born in 1784 in York Co, PA. She married Henry Rohrbach. He was born in 1778.

     v.   Maria Magdalena "Molly" Miller (daughter of Andrew Miller and Anna Maria Hamm) was born in 1788 in York Co, PA. She married Samuel Wehrly.

     vi. John Miller (son of Andrew Miller and Anna Maria Hamm) was born in 1790 in York Co, PA.

     vii. Salome "Sarah" Miller (daughter of Andrew Miller and Anna Maria Hamm) was born in 1793 in PA. She married David Rohrbach. He was born in 1789 in York Co, PA.

     viii. David Miller (son of Andrew Miller and Anna Maria Hamm) was born in 1795 in York Co, PA.

120. **John Nicholas Geib** was born in 1730 in Germany[232]. He died in 1782 in Hellam, York Co, PA[233]. He married **Anna Charlotte Dietz** in 1754 in York, York Co, PA[234].

121. **Anna Charlotte Dietz** was born in 1733 in PA[234, 235]. She died about Abt. 1782 in York Co, PA[236].

More About John Nicholas Geib:

Burial: 1782
Immigration: Bef. 1750
Religion: ; Lutheran[232]
Residence: Abt. 1750 in Hempfield, Lancaster Co, PA[237]
Residence: Bet. 1762-1763 in Hellam, York Co, PA[238, 239]
Will: November 11, 1782 in Hellam, York Co, PA[240, 241, 242, 243]

Notes for John Nicholas Geib:
Gipe, Geib: Probably a respelling of German Geib, a surname of uncertain origin from the Palatinate; according to Bahlow it is a topographic name from a term denoting dirt or decay. German: from an old word for 'dirt', 'grime', presumably applied as a derogatory nickname.

More About Anna Charlotte Dietz:
Religion: ; Reformed[244]

Notes for Anna Charlotte Dietz:
aka surname Or

Anna Charlotte Dietz and John Nicholas Geib had the following children:

        i.   Peter Gipe (son of John Nicholas Geib and Anna Charlotte Dietz) was born in 1755 in York Co, PA. He married Barbara ?. She was born about Abt. 1760.

        ii.   Henry Gipe (son of John Nicholas Geib and Anna Charlotte Dietz) was born in 1756 in York Co, PA. He died in 1841. He married Anna Catherine Lantz. She was born about Abt. 1760.

60.   iii. Jacob Gipe (son of John Nicholas Geib and Anna Charlotte Dietz) was born about Abt. 1761 in York Co, PA[134]. He died on December 18, 1843 in Chanceford, York Co, PA[134, 187]. He married Elizabeth ? about Abt. 1782 in York Co, PA. She was born about Abt. 1762[134]. She died between 1810-1820 in York Co, PA[134]. He married Temperance ?. She was born in 1790.

iv. Anna Catherine Gipe (daughter of John Nicholas Geib and Anna Charlotte Dietz) was born in 1765 in PA. She married Michael King. He was born about Abt. 1760.

v. Eva Gipe (daughter of John Nicholas Geib and Anna Charlotte Dietz) was born about Abt. 1770 in PA.

vi. Margaret Gipe (daughter of John Nicholas Geib and Anna Charlotte Dietz) was born about Abt. 1770 in PA.

vii. Nicholas Gipe (son of John Nicholas Geib and Anna Charlotte Dietz) was born about Abt. 1770 in PA.

viii. Anna Maria Gipe (daughter of John Nicholas Geib and Anna Charlotte Dietz) was born about Abt. 1780 in PA. She married Peter Ditty.

ix. Maria Elizabeth Gipe (daughter of John Nicholas Geib and Anna Charlotte Dietz) was born about Abt. 1781 in PA. She married Peter Kline.

Sources

1 Duncan family information, Jack Lehman, North Charleston, SC.
2 William Duncan, April 1978, PA, Social Security Death Index, www.familysearch.org.
3 Irvin Francis Duncan, Birth record, Northumberland Co County Courthouse, Register of Wills, Sunbury, PA.
4 Irvin Duncan, April 1978, PA, Social Security Death Index, www.familysearch.org.
5 Irvin Francis Duncan death certificate, #0030831, Northumberland Co, PA, Department of Vital Records, New Castle, PA.
6 Mary Lucetta Anderson, Memoranda, Bob Anderson, PA, rmorris@ptd.net.
7 Mamie Duncan, April 1989, PA, Social Security Death Index, www.familysearch.org.
8 Mamie Lucetta Duncan death certificate, #0078833, #069201, April 1989, Department of Vital Record, New Castle, PA.
9 Mamie Luzetta Anderson, #061660-1908, 04-13-1908, Northumberland Co, PA, Department of Vital Records, New Castle, PA.

10 Mamie L Duncan, Probate file, 47-89-85, microfiche, Montour County Courthouse, Office of the Reg and Recorder, Danville, PA, Norman Nicol, ndnicol@epix.net, Mar 2008.

11 Irvin Duncan, Pomfret Manor Cemetery, Sam Derr, Sunbury, PA, lot 130-B.

12 Duncan household, 1910 United States Census, Northumberland Co, PA, ED 0118, Visit 0155, ancestry.com & Microfilm, PA State Library, Hbg, PA.

13 Willard household, 1920 United States Census, Northumberland Co, PA, Roll T625 1611, p 7A, ED 134, Image 0913, ancestry.com & Microfilm, PA State Library, Hbg, PA.

14 Duncan household, 1910 United States Census, Northumberland Co, PA, ED 0118, Visit 0155, ancestry.com & Microfilm, PA State Library, Hbg, PA.

15 Willard household, 1920 United States Census, Northumberland Co, PA, Roll T625 1611, p 7A, ED 134, Image 0913, ancestry.com & Microfilm, PA State Library, Hbg, PA.

16 Irvin Wilfred Francis Duncan, Funeral death record, Olley-Gotlob Funeral Home, Sunbury, PA.

17 Irvin W Duncan, Social Seurity numident record, application for SS-5, SSA, Nov 2006, Baltimore, MD.

18 Irvin Francis Duncan death certificate, Funeral death record, Olley-Gotlob Funeral Home, Sunbury, PA.

19 Mamie Duncan, Pomfret Manor Cemetery, Sam Derr, Sunbury, PA, lot 130-B.

20 Anderson household, 1910 United States Census, Northumberland Co, PA, ED 0115, Sheet 17A, ancestry.com & Microfilm, PA State Library, Hbg, PA.

21 Anderson household, 1920 United States Census, Snyder Co, PA, Roll T625 1653, p 3B, ED 163, Image 0148, www.ancestry.com and 1920 United States Census, Snyder Co, PA, PA State Library microfilm image.

22 Anderson household, 1920 United States Census, Snyder Co, PA, Roll T625 1653, p 3B, ED 163, Image 0148, www.ancestry.com and 1920 United States Census, Snyder Co, PA, PA State Library microfilm image.

23 Mamie L Duncan, Social Seurity numident record, application for SS-5, SSA, Nov 2006, Baltimore, MD.

24 Mamie Lucetta Duncan, #0078833, #069201, April 1989, Department of Vital Record, New Castle, PA.

25 Mamie Duncan, #0078833, #069201, April 1989, Department of Vital Record, New Castle, PA.

26 Duncan-Layman mariage record, #8855, Northumberland Co, PA, 1899, Northumberland Co County Register of Wills.

27 Wm Duncan death certificate, #0030852, #90924, Northumberland Co, PA, Department of Vital records, New Castle, PA.

28 Duncan family information, Stephanie Gormley.

29 Duncan-Layman marriage record, April 20, 1899, Edward C. Eisley.

30 Duncan-Layman marriage record, #8855, Northumberland Co, PA, 1899, Northumberland Co County Register of Wills, Sunbury, PA.

31 Duncan-Layman marriage record, #8855, Northumberland Co, PA, 1899, Northumberland Co County Register of Wills.

32 Lottie V. Willard, death certificate, File #29987, Reg #19, #3505042, February 1936, Department of Vital Records, New Castle, PA.

33 William Duncan, Pomfret Manor Cemetery, Sunbury, Northumberland Co, PA, NCHS, The Hunter House, Sunbury, PA.

34 William Duncan, Northumberland Co County, Pennsylvania, 1851-92, Zion Evangelical Church, www.ancestry.com.

35 William Duncan, Baptisms of Infants, Zion Evan Luth Register, 1851-1892, Sunbury, PA, p41.

36 Wm Duncan death certificate, #0030852, #90924, Northumberland Co, PA, Department of Vital records, New Castle, PA.

37 William Duncan, Pomfret Manor Cemetery, Sam Derr, Sunbury, PA, lot 130-B.

38 Donkert household, 1880 United States Census, Northumberland Co, PA, ancestry.com & Microfilm, PA State Library, Hbg, PA.

39 Duncan household, 1900 United States Census, microfilm image, PA State Library.

40 Wm Duncan, Northumberland Co County Courthouse, Register of Wills, 11-27-1901.

41 William Duncan, Probate files, July 1906, Northumberland County Courthouse, Reg of Wills, Bk 12, p424, Sunbury, PA, Robyn Jackson, genealogylover@msn.com, 2008.

42 Duncan household, 1900 United States Census, microfilm image, PA State Library.
Died Sunbury, PA, Duncan family information, Stephanie Gormley.

43 Charlotte Layman, Duncan family information, Stephanie Gormley.

44 Lottie Duncan, Pomfret Manor Cemetery, Sam Derr, Sunbury, PA, lot 130-B.

45 Lottie V. Willard, Lottie Duncan, Pomfret Manor Cemetery, Sam Derr, Sunbury, PA, lot 130-B.

46 Willard household, 1930 United States Census, Northumberland Co, PA, Roll T626 2091, p 7A, ED 71, Image 0681, ancestry.com & Microfilm, PA State Library, Hbg, PA.

47 Lottie V Willard death certificate, File #29987, Reg #19, #3505042, February 1936, Department of Vital Records, New Castle, PA.

48 Willard household, 1930 United States Census, Northumberland Co, PA, Roll T626 2091, p 7A, ED 71, Image 0681, ancestry.com & Microfilm, PA State Library, Hbg, PA.

49 Catherine Duncan, Death certificate, Northumberland Co County Register of Wills, Sunbury, PA.

50 Dungard household, 1870 United States Census, Northumberland Co, PA, ancestry.com & Microfilm, PA State Library, Hbg, PA.

51 Dungan household, 1870 United States Census, Northumberland Co, PA, ancestry.com & Microfilm, PA State Library, Hbg, PA.

52 Dungard household, 1870 United States Census, Northumberland Co, PA, ancestry.com & Microfilm, PA State Library, Hbg, PA.

53 Donkert household, 1880 United States Census, Northumberland Co, PA, ancestry.com & Microfilm, PA State Library, Hbg, PA.

54 Duncan family information, Stephanie Gormley, PA, 1989.

55 McCloud household, 1860 United States Census, Northumberland Co, PA, ancestry.com & Microfilm, PA State Library, Hbg, PA.

56 Donkert household, 1880 United States Census, Northumberland Co, PA, FHL 1255164, Film T9-1164, p 521B, www.familysearch.org.

57 Melinda Duncan, Cemetery record, Apr 1933, A genealogists Guide to Burials in Northumberland Co, PA, Vol I, Meiser & Meiser, 1989.

58 Sallie Duncan, Cemetery record, Apr 1933, A genealogists Guide to Burials in Northumberland Co, PA, Vol I, Meiser & Meiser, 1989.

59 Sarah Duncan, Baptisms of Infants, Zion Evan Luth Register, 1851-1892, Sunbury, PA, p41.

60 Hannah Artilla Duncan, Baptisms of Infants, Zion Evan Luth Register, 1851-1892, Sunbury, PA, p94.

61 Charley Duncan, Baptisms of Infants, Zion Evan Luth Register, 1851-1892, Sunbury, PA, p101.

62 Layman/Lehman family information, Files, NCHS, The Hunter House, Sunbury, PA.

63 Joseph Pierce Layman, death record, Illinois Statewide Death Index, 1916-1950, www.cyberdriveillinois.com/GenealogyMWeb/ODPHdeathsearch.

64 Joseph Pierce Layman, State of IL, Dept of Public Health, DVS, Reg #4976, Primary Dt #3104, Cook, IL, Feb 1924.

65 Lehman-Oberlander marriage, source unknown.

66 Rebecca Lehman (Layman) death certificate, #105066, Reg # 456, #3457529, Novemrber 1921, Department of Vital Records, New Castle, PA.

67 Joseph P Leyman, Evergreen Cemtery, Index files and lot lists, #5435, Lot SG 157, Maple Gr Pt 6, vault 5/9/box, permit #4976, Chiacgo, IL.

68 Lyman household, 1860 United States Census, York Co, PA, ancestry.com & Microfilm, PA State Library, Hbg, PA.

69 Lyman household, 1870 United States Census, York Co, PA, Roll M593 1468, p 545, Image 700, ancestry.com & Microfilm, PA State Library, Hbg, PA.

70 Hawkins household, 1900 United States Census, Northumberland Co, PA, ancestry.com & Microfilm, PA State Library, Hbg, PA.

71 Hawkins household, 1920 United States Census, Cook, IL, ancestry.com & Microfilm, PA State Library, Hbg, PA.

72 Lyman household, 1870 United States Census, York Co, PA, Roll M593-1468, p 545, Image 700, ancestry.com & Microfilm, PA State Library, Hbg, PA.

73 Laynon household, 1900 United States Census, Northumberland Co, PA, ancestry.com & Microfilm, PA State Library, Hbg, PA.

74 Rebecca Layman, Pomfret Manor Cemetery, Sam Derr, Sunbury, PA, lot 130-B.

75 Oberlander household, 1870 United States Census, York Co, PA, Roll M593-1468, p 227, Image 67, ancestry.com & Microfilm, PA State Library, Hbg, PA.

76 Laymen household, 1910 United States Census, Northumberland Co, PA, ED 0114, Visit 0085, ancestry.com & Microfilm, PA State Library, Hbg, PA.

77 Oberlander household, 1870 United States Census, York Co, PA, ancestry.com & Microfilm, PA State Library, Hbg, PA.

78 Laymen household, 1910 United States Census, Northumberland Co, PA, ED 0114, Visit 0085, ancestry.com & Microfilm, PA State Library, Hbg, PA.

79 David McCloud, Probate files, 1864, Northumberland County Courthouse, Reg of Wills, Sunbury, Bk 5, p261, PA, Robyn Jackson, genealogylover@msn.com, 2008.

80 McLeod household, 1850 United States Census, Northumberland Co, PA, ancestry.com & Microfilm, PA State Library, Hbg, PA.

81 McCloud household, 1860 United States Census, Northumberland Co, PA, Series M653, Roll 1149, p 71, ancestry.com & Microfilm, PA State Library, Hbg, PA.

82 McLeod household, 1850 United States Census, Northumberland Co, PA, ancestry.com & Microfilm, PA State Library, Hbg, PA.

83 McCloud household, 1860 United States Census, Northumberland Co, PA, Series M653, Roll 1149, p 71, ancestry.com & Microfilm, PA State Library, Hbg, PA.

84 McCloud household, 1870 United States Census, Northumberland Co, PA, ancestry.com & Microfilm, PA State Library, Hbg, PA.

85 McCloud household, 1880 United States Census, Northumberland Co, PA, ancestry.com & Microfilm, PA State Library, Hbg, PA.

86 McCloud household, 1880 United States Census, Northumberland Co, PA, ancestry.com & Microfilm, PA State Library, Hbg, PA.

87 McCloud household, 1870 United States Census, Northumberland Co, PA, ancestry.com & Microfilm, PA State Library, Hbg, PA.

88 McCloud-Frye, Marriage, Northumberland County, SS, #2856, Register & Recorder, Sunbury, PA, Oct 1890, Market St, Sunbury, PA.

89 Michael Layman, Bethel ME Cemetery, p 151, Jerome K. Hively, Brogue, PA.

90 Elmira Layman, Bethel ME Cemetery, p 151, Jerome K. Hively, Brogue, PA.

91 Lyman household, 1850 United States Census, York Co, PA, Roll M432-839, p 206, Image 180, ancestry.com & Microfilm, PA State Library, Hbg, PA.

92 Lyman household, 1870 United States Census, York Co, PA, Roll M593-1468, p 545, Image 700, ancestry.com & Microfilm, PA State Library, Hbg, PA.

93 Lyman household, 1880 United States Census, York Co, PA, FHL 1255208, Film T9-1208, p 640D, www.familysearch.org.

94 Lyman household, 1860 United States Census, York Co, PA, ancestry.com & Microfilm, PA State Library, Hbg, PA.

95 Leyman family information, source unknown.

96 Duncan family information, 1870 United States Census, York Co, PA, Roll M593-1468, p 545, Image 700, ancestry.com & Microfilm, PA State Library, Hbg, PA.

97 Overlander-Kipe marriage record, #662-59, Calender of Vital Records of the Counties of York & Adams.

98 Sarah Oberlander, Probate files, 1874, Rep 42, York County Archives, York, PA, Deborah Hershey, Elizabethtown, PA, Dec 2008.

99 Oberlander household, 1830 United States Census, York Co, PA, ancestry.com & Microfilm, PA State Library, Hbg, PA.

100 Oberlander household, 1840 United States Census, York Co, PA, ancestry.com & Microfilm, PA State Library, Hbg, PA.

101 Oberlander household, 1850 United States Census, York Co, PA, Roll M432 839, p 839, ancestry.com & Microfilm, PA State Library, Hbg, PA.

102 Oberlander household, 1860 United States Census, York Co, PA, ancestry.com & Microfilm, PA State Library, Hbg, PA.

103 Oberlander household, 1870 United States Census, York Co, PA, ancestry.com & Microfilm, PA State Library, Hbg, PA.

104 Oberlander household, 1880 United States Census, York Co, PA, ancestry.com & Microfilm, PA State Library, Hbg, PA.

105 Oberlander household, 1850 United States Census, York Co, PA, Roll M432 839, p 839, ancestry.com & Microfilm, PA State Library, Hbg, PA.

106 Oberlander household, 1860 United States Census, York Co, PA, ancestry.com & Microfilm, PA State Library, Hbg, PA.

107 Oberlander household, 1880 United States Census, York Co, PA, FHL 1255207, Film T9-1207, p 599C, www.familysearch.org.

108 Sarah Oberlander, Probate files, 1874, Rep 42, Bk 342, York County Archives, York, PA, Deborah Hershey, Elizabethtown, PA, Dec 2008.

109 Lehman-Klein marriage record, June 28, 1818, Church Book records 4.

110 Lehman-Klein marriage record, Marriages at Trinity Lutheran Church, Lancaster Co, PA, Joan E. Kahler, Charles.Kahler@worldnet.att.net.

111 David R. Layman, Biography, source unknown.

112 Layman household, 1800 United States Census, Centre Co, PA, ancestry.com & Microfilm, PA State Library, Hbg, PA.

113 Layman household, 1810 United States Census, Centre Co, PA, ancestry.com & Microfilm, PA State Library, Hbg, PA.

114 Klein hosusehold, 1820 United States Census, Lancaster Co, PA, ancestry.com & Microfilm, PA State Library, Hbg, PA.

115 Rieman household, 1820 United States Census, York Co, PA, ancestry.com & Microfilm, PA State Library, Hbg, PA.

116 John Reiman, York Co, PA Will index, c/o Gert Mysliwski, gert@foothill.net.

117 Michael Oberland, 1798, #3, York County Births 1730-1900, Humphrey, Gert Mysliwski,gert@foothill.net.

118 Michael Oberland, St. Matthews Lutheran Church records, Hanover, PA, Helda Kline.

119 Warner family information, JWerner.txt, Don Varner, DRVarner@aol.com.

120 Maria Catharina Werner, baptismal record, St Jacobs Lutheran Church, Vicki Kessler, Secretary, saintjacobslutheranchurch@msn.com.

121 Michael Oberlander, findagrave.com.

122 Oberlander household, 1800 United States Census, York Co, PA, ancestry.com & Microfilm, PA State Library, Hbg, PA.

123 Oberlander household, 1810 United States Census, York Co, PA, ancestry.com & Microfilm, PA State Library, Hbg, PA.

124 Overlander household, 1830 United States Census, York Co, PA, ancestry.com & Microfilm, PA State Library, Hbg, PA.

125 Overlander household, 1840 United States Census, York Co, PA, ancestry.com & Microfilm, PA State Library, Hbg, PA.

126 Oberlander household, 1850 United States Census, York Co, PA, ancestry.com & Microfilm, PA State Library, Hbg, PA.

127 Oberlander household, 1880 United States Census, York Co, PA, www.ancestry.com and 1880 United States Census, York Co, PA, FHL 1255207, Film T9-1207, p 599C, www.familysearch.org.

128 Oberlander household, 1850 United States Census, York Co, PA, ancestry.com & Microfilm, PA State Library, Hbg, PA.

129 Oberlander household, 1880 United States Census, York Co, PA, ancestry.com & Microfilm, PA State Library, Hbg, PA and 1880 United States Census, York Co, PA, FHL 1255207, Film T9-1207, p 599C, www.familysearch.org.

130 Maria Catherine Werner, St. Jacobs (Stone) UCC Church, Doris Miller, Glenville, PA.

131 Maria Catharine Warner Oberlander, findagave.com.

132 Warner household, 1800 United States Census, York Co, PA, ancestry.com & Microfilm, PA State Library, Hbg, PA.

133 Warner household, 1810 United States Census, York Co, PA, ancestry.com & Microfilm, PA State Library, Hbg, PA.

134 Gipe Family of Chanceford Twp., York Co, 1997, Harry A. Diehl, p 1-5.

135 Gipe household, 1810 United States Census, York Co, PA, ancestry.com & Microfilm, PA State Library, Hbg, PA.

136 Gipe household, 1820 United States Census, York Co, PA, ancestry.com & Microfilm, PA State Library, Hbg, PA.

137 Geipe household, 1830 United States Census, York Co, PA, ancestry.com & Microfilm, PA State Library, Hbg, PA.

138 Gipe household, 1840 United States Census, York Co, PA, Joanne Murry, rootsweb.com.

139 Gibe household, 1850 United States Census, York Co, PA, Roll M432-839, p 40, Image 648, ancestry.com & Microfilm, PA State Library, Hbg, PA.

140 Michael Leyman, Commemorative Biographical Record, Northern PA.

141 Michael Leyman, Baptism/Birth, Southeastern Pennsylvania, 1600-1800 Index, Fillows4@aol.com.

142 Michael Leyman, Howard Cemetery, Centre Co, PA, p 5.

143 Rachel Leyman, Howard Cemetery, Centre Co, PA, p 5.

144 Limmen household, 1790 United States Census, Northumberland Co, PA ancestry.com & Microfilm, PA State Library, Hbg, PA.

145 Lausman household, 18000 United States Census, Northumberland Co, PA, Roll M32-37, p 852, Image 200, ancestry.com.

146 Lyman household, 1810 United States Census, Centre Co, PA, ancestry.com & Microfilm, PA State Library, Hbg, PA.

147 Lyman household, 1820 United States Census, Centre Co, PA, ancestry.com & Microfilm, PA State Library, Hbg, PA.

148 Lymon household, 1830 United States Census, Centre Co, PA, Roll M19 165, p 433, Image 849, ancestry.com & Microfilm, PA State Library, Hbg, PA.

149 Leyman household, 1840 United States Census, Centre Co, PA, ancestry.com & Microfilm, PA State Library, Hbg, PA.

150 Mich. Leman, Commonwealth of PA, PA Historical & Museum Society.

151 George H Leyman, Commemorative Biographical Record, p 871-872.

152 Leyman family information, Tax list, 1796, West Buffalo, Northumberland (Union) Co, PA.

153 Michael Lyman, Union Co, PA Tax list, 1796, Annals of Buffalo Valley, p 393.

154 Michael Layman, List of Taxables, p 318, Jack Lehman, North Charleston, SC.

155 Michael Lyman, List of Taxable Inhabitants, Centre Twp., 1810.

156 Lyman household, 1820 United States Census, Centre Co, PA, ancestry.com & Microfilm, PA State Library, Hbg, PA.

157 Michael Leyman, Probate file, 2723, 9pp, microfiche, Centre Co, PA Reg of Wills, Bellefonte, PA, Norman Nicol, ndnicol@epix.net, Mar 2008.

158 Mich. Leman, April 26, 1781, Commonwealth of PA, PA Historical & Museum Society.

159 Leyman family information, Tax list, 1796, West Buffalo, Northumberland (Union) Co, PA.

160 Leyman family information, Tax list, 1799, Mifflinburg, Union Co, PA.

161 George H Layman, Commemorative Biographical Record of Cental PA, vol 1, Beers and Co, 1898, Jack Lehman, North Charleston, SC.

162 Michael Leyman, January 2, 1843, May 10, 1843, Copy of Will, Register of Wills, Centre County, PA.

163 Layman household, 1850 United States Census, Centre Co, PA, ancestry.com & Microfilm, PA State Library, Hbg, PA.

164 Layman household, 1850 United States Census, Centre Co, PA, ancestry.com & Microfilm, PA State Library, Hbg, PA.

165 Henry Klein, WFT, Volume 43, Tree 971.

166 Kline household, 1810 United States Census, Lancaster Co, PA, ancestry.com & Microfilm, PA State Library, Hbg, PA.

167 Kline household, 1820 United States Census, Lancaster Co, PA, ancestry.com & Microfilm, PA State Library, Hbg, PA.

168 Kline household, 1830 United States Census, Lancaster Co, PA, ancestry.com.

169 Henry Klein, June 18, 1832, December 1832, Abstracts of Lancaster County Wills, Lancaster Co, PA.

170 Henry Klein, History of Lancaster County, F Ellis & S Evans, p 960, Lancaster County Historical Society.

171 Peter Overlander, World Tree, awt.ancestry.com/cgi-bin/sse.dll, www.ancestry.com.

172 Jacob Oberlander, Saul/Kagy/Weisenauer/gqinner Family, Mary Ross, ross.8@osu.edu, awt.ancestry.com/.

173 Overlander-Baugher marriage, Hanover, PA, Christie Fleming, CFleming@eagle.org.

174 Overland household, 1800 United States Census, York Co, PA, Roll M32 44, p 1351, Image 183, ancestry.com & Microfilm, PA State Library, Hbg, PA.

175 Jacob Oberlander, 1816, Probate Invent. Index York County, PA, 1749-1850, Chanceford, York County, PA, Gert Mysliwski,gert@foothill.net.

176 Jacob Oberlander, Probate files, 1816, Rep 39, York County Archives, York, PA, Deborah Hershey, Elizabethtown, PA, Dec 2008.

177 Johann Christian Werner, #262-385, Calender of Vitals records of the Counties of York & Adams Co.

178 Johann Christian Werner, St. Jacobs (Stone) UCC Church, Doris Miller, Glenville, PA.

179 Miller Family information, Jean M. Sterner, Spring Grove, PA 17362.

180 Johann Christian Werner, 1775, St. Jacobs Lutheran & Reformed Church, Codorus, York Co, PA, Early York County Births, J. Humphrey.

181 Warner household, 1810 United States Census, York Co, PA, Roll M252 57, p 207, Image 218, ancestry.com & Microfilm, PA State Library, Hbg, PA.

182 Warner household, 1820 United States Census, York Co, PA, ancestry.com & Microfilm, PA State Library, Hbg, PA.

183 Warner household, 1830 United States Census, York Co, PA, ancestry.com & Microfilm, PA State Library, Hbg, PA.

184 Warner household, 1840 United States Census, York Co, PA, ancestry.com & Microfilm, PA State Library, Hbg, PA.

185 Johann Christian Warner, March 10, 1840, June 22, 1842, bk s, p 255.

186 Warner household, 1850 United States Census, York Co, PA, ancestry.com & Microfilm, PA State Library, Hbg, PA.

187 Jacob Gipe, 1844, Probate Invent. Index York County, PA, 1749-1850, Chanceford, York County, PA, Gert Mysliwski,gert@foothill.net.

188 Geipe household, 1830 United States Census, York Co, PA ancestry.com & Microfilm, PA State Library, Hbg, PA.

189 Gipe household, 1840 United States Census, York Co, PA, ancestry.com & Microfilm, PA State Library, Hbg, PA.

190 Jacob Gipe, April 4, 1844, bk 20, p 444, Will Records, York County, PA.

191 Jacob Gipe, Probate files, 1845, Rep 36, York County Archives, York, PA, Deborah Hershey, Elizabethtown, PA, Dec 2008.

192 Jacob Gype, Tax list, 1783, Windsor, York County, PA.

193 Johann Jacob Leiman, Passenger and Immigration Lists Index, 1500-1900, myfamily.com, P. William Filby, ancestry.com.

194 Joahnn Jacob Leiman, PA Census, 1772-1890, Philadelphia, PA, www.ancestry.com.

195 Jacob Loyman, Probate files, Bk E, vol 1, p196, Lancaster County Archives Division, Lancaster Co Courthouse, Lancaster, PA, Deborah Hershey, Elizabethtown, PA, Mar 2008.

196 Margaret Layman, Estate Inventory, 1786, b86, f8, Marge Bardeen, 2006, Lancaster County Historical Society, Lancaster, PA.

197 Peter Klein, Abstract of Lancaster County Wills, Lancaster County Historical Society.

198 Peter Michael Klein, Probate files, Bk I, Vol 1, p269, Archives Div, Lancaster Co Courthouse, Lancaster, PA.

199 Peter Oberlander, Probate files, loose files, Lancaster County Archives Division, Lancaster Co Courthouse, Lancaster, PA, Deborah Hershey, Elizabethtown, PA, Mar 2008.

200 Pedro Oberlander, Passenger and Immigration Lists Index, 1500-1900, myfamily.com, P. William Filby, ancestry.com.

201 Oberlander family information, PA Births, Lebanon County, J. Humphrey.

202 Pedro Oberlander, PA Census, 1772-1890, Philadelphia, PA, www.ancestry.com.

203 William Bager, World Tree, awt.ancestry.com/cgi-bin/sse.dll, www.ancestry.com.

204 Baugher family information, Kim Morris.

205 George William Baugher, Conrad Maul & and his Descendants, p 285, Adams Co County Historical Society.

206 Baugher household, 1790 United States Census, York Co, PA, Roll M637-9, p 288, Image 0237, ancestry.com & Microfilm, PA State Library, Hbg, PA.

207 John George Bager (father), Passenger and Immigration Lists Index, 1500-1900, myfamily.com, P. William Filby, ancestry.com.

208 Baugher family information, Tax lists 1779, 1780, 1781, 1782, 1783, York Co, PA, Kim Morris.

209 Wm Baugher, September 9, 1775, Land record, #11766, Berwick, York Co, PA.

210 John Bager, York County, PA Wills, 1749-1819, www.ancestry.com.

211 William Bauger, April 18, 1798, May 17, 1798, Probate Invent. Index York County, PA, 1749-1850, Berwick, Adams Co County, PA, Gert gert@foothill.net.

212 Wolliam (sic) Baugher, April 18, 1798, May 17, 1798, Will Abstracts of York County, PA, 1749-1819, Gert Mysliwski,gert@foothill.net.

213 Warner household, 1790 United States Census, York Co, PA, Roll M637 9, p 284, Image 0221, ancestry.com & Microfilm, PA State Library, Hbg, PA.

214 John Werner, Probate files, 1805, Rep 47, York County Archives, York, PA, Deborah Hershey, Elizabethtown, PA, Dec 2008.

215 John Werner, July 20, 1805, August 16, 1805, Abstracts of York County Wills 1749-1819, Family Line Publication, 1995, L. Gohn lbeth@erols.com.

216 Andreas Miller, Miller family, Onetree, ancestry.com.

217 Andrew Miller, 1842, York County Archives, York Co, PA.

218 Miller family information, Julie Azzalina, indyboy@email.msn.com.

219 Andrew Miller, Probate files, 1842, Rep 338 York County Archives, York, PA, Deborah Hershey, Elizabethtown, PA, Dec 2008.

220 Anna Maria Hamm, November 10, 1763, Christ Reformed, Littlestown, York (Adams) Co, PA.

221 Miller family information, Jean M. Sterner, Spring Grove, PA 17362.

222 Miller household, 1790 United States Census, York Co, PA, Roll M637 9, p 270, Image 0204, ancestry.com & Microfilm, PA State Library, Hbg, PA.

223 Miller household, 1810 United States Census, York Co, PA, ancestry.com & Microfilm, PA State Library, Hbg, PA.

224 Miller household, 1820 United States Census, York Co, PA, ancestry.com & Microfilm, PA State Library, Hbg, PA.

225 Miller household, 1830 United States Census, York Co, PA, ancestry.com & Microfilm, PA State Library, Hbg, PA.

226 Miller household, 1840 United States Census, York Co, PA, ancestry.com & Microfilm, PA State Library, Hbg, PA.

227 Andrew Miller, 1841 Rev War Census Ensuf Pensioner of PA, Eastern Dt, p 116, Barbara, homelybin@aol.com.

228 Andrew Miller, PA Census,1772-1890 Record, PA 1840 Pensioners List, Ronald V Jackson, AIS, ancestry.com.

229 12,000 Ancestors, Andrew Miller, reseracher Wonders waht's ahppended to her 12,000 relatives, June R Grove, Caryl Clarke, http://w2.ydr.com/story/security/74736/.

230 Andrew Miller, Probate files, 1842, Rep 38, York County Archives, York, PA, Deborah Hershey, Elizabethtown, PA, Dec 2008.

231 Anna Maria Hamm, January 1, 1764, Christ Reformed, Littlestown, York (Adams) Co, PA.

232 Geip family information, December 9, 1992, Philip O'Leary, Willowick, OH 44095.

233 Gipe/Geib/Geiep,York Co, PA, Phil O'Leary.

234 Anna Charlotte Or, One tree, from WFT collection, trees.ancestry.com/owt, www.ancestry.com.

235 June Delores Gerrick Pedigree Chart, June G Herr, 7501 15th Avenue N, St. Petersburg, FL 33710.

236 Johan Nicholas Geipp, Geipp family, Onetree, ancestry.com.

237 Gipe family information, Harry A. Diehl, Wilmington, DE.

238 Nicolas Gipe, Tax list, 1762, Hellam, York County, PA.

239 Nicholas Gype, Tax list, 1763, Hellam, York County, PA.

240 Nicholas Geip, Sr., 1782, bk F, p 57, May 28, 1776, November 11, 1782, York County, PA Wills, 1749-1819, York County, PA, www.ancestry.com.

Sources (con't)

241 Nicolas Geip Jr, 1782, F-57, May 28, 1776, November 11, York County, PA Wills, 1749-1819, York County, PA, Gert Mysliwski,gert@foothill.net.

242 Nicholas Geip, Sr., May 28, 1776, November 11, 1782, Will Abstracts of York County, PA, 1749-1819, Gert Mysliwski,gert@foothill.net.

243 Nicholas Geib, Probate files, 1782, Rep 35, #436, York County Archives, York, PA, Deborah Hershey, Elizabethtown, PA, Dec 2008.

244 Geipp-Schreiberin marriage record, Trinity Lutheran Church, Lancaster Co, PA German Society, volume VII, p 235.

Chapter Two

Our family's photos.

Some photographs of our family.
A picture is worth a thousand words.

Photos of Irvin Duncan

Irvin Wilfred Duncan

Birth:	November 27, 1901	Father:	William Duncan
Death:	April 08, 1978	Mother:	Charlotte "Lottie" Virginia Layman
Marriage:	June 07, 1926	Spouse:	Mary "Mamie" Lucetta Anderson

6 Irvin Duncan c1908, bottom row, 2nd from left

6 Irvin Duncan c1928, Patricia Duncan, Retta, Bud, Mamie, Ethel, Irvin, Harry Duncan Jr

6 Irvin Duncan c1930, on right

6 Irvin Duncan c1935

6 Irvin Duncan c1938, Ethel & Shirley Duncan, Mamie Anderson, Bud, Irvin & Lenore Duncan

6 Irvin Duncan c1945

6 Irvin Duncan c1952

6 Irvin Duncan c1960 & Mamie Anderson

6 Irvin Duncan c1970

6 Irvin Duncan c1970 & Mamie Anderson (2)

6 Irvin Duncan c1975 & Mamie Anderson (3)

Photos of William Duncan

William Duncan

Birth:	January 16, 1876	Father:	Frederick (Fritz Dankert) Duncan
Death:	September 11, 1906	Mother:	Catherine McCloud
Marriage:	April 13, 1899	Spouse:	Charlotte "Lottie" Virginia Layman

12 William Duncan c1905

12 William Duncan c1905 (3)

12 William Duncan c1905 (4)

12 William Duncan c1905, & Charlotte Layman(2)

Photos of Charlotte Layman

Charlotte "Lottie" Virginia Layman

Birth:	May 12, 1879	Father:	Joseph Pierce Layman
Death:	February 29, 1936	Mother:	Rebecca Jane Overlander
Marriage:	April 13, 1899	Spouse:	William Duncan

13 Charlotte Layman
c1905

13 Charlotte Layman
c1905 & Irvin Duncan

13 Charlotte Layman
c1926, Mamie Anderson,
Charlotte Layman & child

13 Charlotte Layman
c1928, Bud, Mamie
Anderson, Charlotte
Layman, Ethel & woman
w.child

13 Charlotte Layman
c1930, Mamie Anderson,
Charlotte Layman & Irvin
Duncan

Photos of Rebecca Overlander

Rebecca Jane Overlander

Birth:	October 1859	Father:	Jacob Warner Oberlander
Death:	November 20, 1921	Mother:	Sarah "Sallie" Ann Gipe
Marriage:	1877	Spouse:	Joseph Pierce Layman

27 Rebecca Oberlander
c1920

Photos of Michael Layman

Michael Layman

Birth:	October 10, 1818		Father:	Michael Layman
Death:	May 17, 1892		Mother:	Sarah Klein
Marriage:	April 03, 1845		Spouse:	Elmira Elizabeth Raymond

52 Michael Layman 1892

Photos of Elmira Raymond

Elmira Elizabeth Raymond

Birth:	January 17, 1824	Father:	John Reiman
Death:	November 05, 1888	Mother:	Nancy? ?
Marriage:	April 03, 1845	Spouse:	Michael Layman

53 Elmira Raymond 1888

Photos of William Bager

John George William Bager

Birth:	April 15, 1750	Father:	
Death:	May 17, 1798	Mother:	
Marriage:	Abt. 1770	Spouse:	Eva Catherine Kepner

1380 John George
Baugher

1380 John George
Baugher (2)

690 John George William
Baugher 1798

Chapter Three

Our family's places.

Where we're from, born, raised, lived
and roamed through and what property
value our ancestors had.

Places

$100
McCloud, David
> Propty: Private

Oberlander, Michael Baugher
> Propty: Private

$100 + $40
McCloud, David
> Propty: Private

$150 + $100
?, Mary
> Propty: Private

$3000 + $2500
Layman, Michael
> Propty: Private

$4000 + $1500
Oberlander, Jacob Warner
> Propty: Private

$4000 + $640
Oberlander, Jacob Warner
> Propty: Private

$450
Neal, Rachel
> Propty: Private

$500
Duncan, Frederick (Fritz Dankert)
> Propty: Private

$600 + $675
Layman, Michael
> Propty: Private

1014 R.R. Ave., Sunbury, Northumberland Co, PA
McCloud, Catherine
> Res: Private

209 3rd St., Sunbury, Northumberland Co, PA
Layman, Joseph Pierce
> Res: Private

517 Chestnut St., Sunbury, Northumberland Co, PA
Overlander, Rebecca Jane
> Res: Private

63 8th St., Sunbury, Northumbelrand, PA
Duncan, Irvin Wilfred
> Res: Private

63 8th St., Sunbury, Northumberland Co, PA
Layman, Charlotte "Lottie" Virginia

63 8th St., Sunbury, Northumberland Co, PA (con't)
    Res: Private

908 W 70th St, Chicago, Cook Co, IL
    Layman, Joseph Pierce
        Res: Private

918 Susquehanna Ave., Sunbury, Northumberland, PA
    Duncan, William
        Res: Private

920 Susquehanna Ave., Sunbury, Northumberland Co, PA
    Duncan, Irvin Wilfred
        Res: Private
    Duncan, William
        Res: Private
    Layman, Charlotte "Lottie" Virginia
        Res: Private

927 Railroad Ave., Sunbury, Northumberland Co, PA
    McCloud, Catherine
        Res: Private

929 Railroad Ave., Sunbury, Northumberland Co, PA
    Duncan, William
        Res: Private

Airville, York Co, PA
    Layman, Joseph Pierce
        Birth: Private

At home, Sunbury, Northumberland Co, PA
    Anderson, Mary "Mamie" Lucetta
        Birth: Private

at Irvin's home, Monroe, Snyder Co, PA
    Layman, Charlotte "Lottie" Virginia
        Death: Private

Augusta, Northumberland Co, PA
    McCloud, David
        Census: Private
        Census: Private

Berwick, York Co, PA
    Bager, John George William
        Death: Private
        Will: Private
        Res: Private
    Baugher, Susan
        Birth: Private
    Kepner, Eva Catherine
        Death: Private
    Oberlander, Jacob
        Birth: Private

Bethel United Methodist, Lower Chanceford, York Co, PA
    Layman, Michael

Bethel United Methodist, Lower Chanceford, York Co, PA (con't)
>Burial: Private

Raymond, Elmira Elizabeth
>Burial: Private

Blackstone Avenue, Chicago, Cook, IL
Layman, Joseph Pierce
>Res: Private

Blue Hill, Dogtown, Jackson, Kantz, Kratzerville, Penn Avon, Salem, Selinsgrove, Verdilla, all Snyder, PA
Duncan, Irvin Wilfred
>Res: Private

Brogueville, York Co, PA
Layman, Charlotte "Lottie" Virginia
>Birth: Private

Buffalo Valley, Lancaster (Union) Co, PA
Neal, Henry
>Birth: Private

Neal, Rachel
>Birth: Private

CA
Masteller, Eula I
>Death: Private

Centre Co, PA
Layman, Michael
>Prob: Private

Centre, Centre Co, PA
Layman, Michael
>Res: Private

Chanceford, York Co, PA
Baugher, Susan
>Death: Private

Gipe, Jacob
>Death: Private
>Census: Private
>Census: Private
>Prob: Private

Gipe, John
>Death: Private
>Census: Private

Gipe, Sarah "Sallie" Ann
>Birth: Private
>Death: Private
>Census: Private
>Census: Private
>Will: Private
>Prob: Private

Layman, Joseph Pierce
>Marr: Private

Miller, Maria Elizabeth

Chanceford, York Co, PA (con't)
> Census: Private

Oberlander, Jacob
>> Death: Private
>> Prob: Private

Oberlander, Jacob Warner
>> Birth: Private
>> Death: Private
>> Census: Private
>> Census: Private
>> Census: Private
>> Census: Private

Oberlander, Michael Baugher
>> Death: Private
>> Census: Private
>> Census: Private
>> Census: Private
>> Census: Private
>> Census: Private

Overlander, Rebecca Jane
>> Birth: Private
>> Marr: Private

Warner, John Christian
>> Census: Private

Warner, Maria Catherine
>> Death: Private

Chanceford, York Co, PA (Rebeck)
Overlander, Rebecca Jane
> Census: Private

Chicago, Cook Co, IL
Layman, Joseph Pierce
>> Death: Private
>> Res: Private

Chicago, Cook, IL
Layman, Joseph Pierce
>> Census: Private

Overlander, Rebecca Jane
>> Census: Private

Christ Lutheran, Elizabethtown, Lancaster Co, PA
Layman, Michael
>> Marr: Private

Raymond, Elmira Elizabeth
>> Marr: Private

Codorus, York Co, PA
?, Judith
>> Death: Private

Miller, Andrew
>> Death: Private
>> Will: Private
>> Census: Private

Codorus, York Co, PA (con't)
              Census: Private
              Census: Private
              Census: Private
              Census: Private
               Prob: Private
      Warner, John Christian
              Census: Private
              Census: Private
      Werner, John George
               Death: Private
                Will: Private
               Prob: Private

Codorus, York Co, PA (Meller)
      Miller, Andrew
              Census: Private

Codorus, York Co, PA w/husband
      Hamm, Anna Maria
              Census: Private

Columbia, Lancaster Co, PA
      Layman, Theodore Augusta
               Birth: Private

Conestoga Tp, Lancaster Co, PA
      Loyman, John Jacob
                Will: Private

Cordorus, York Co, PA
      Miller, Maria Elizabeth
               Birth: Private
              Census: Private
              Census: Private

Dauphin Co, PA
      Reiman, John
               Birth: Private

Democrat
      Anderson, Mary "Mamie" Lucetta
              PoliticalParty: Private

Derry, Montour Co, PA
      Anderson, Mary "Mamie" Lucetta
               Death: Private

Emanuels (Jefferson) Union Cemetery, Jefferson, York Co, PA
      Miller, Andrew
               Burial: Private

Evergreen Cemetery, Chicago, IL
      Layman, Joseph Pierce
               Burial: Private

F.K. Sutton, Selinsgrove, Snyder Co, PA
      Layman, Charlotte "Lottie" Virginia

F.K. Sutton, Selinsgrove, Snyder Co, PA (con't)
> Funeral: Private

father
> Baugher, Susan
>> Census: Private
> Gipe, John
>> Census: Private
>> Census: Private
> Miller, Maria Elizabeth
>> Census: Private
> Oberlander, Michael Baugher
>> Census: Private
>> Census: Private
> Warner, John Christian
>> Census: Private
> Warner, Maria Catherine
>> Census: Private
>> Census: Private

father age 10
> Oberlander, Jacob Warner
>> Census: Private
>> Census: Private

First Trinity Reformed, Chanceford, York Co, PA
> Oberlander, Michael Baugher
>> Marr: Private
> Warner, Maria Catherine
>> Marr: Private

Geisinger Medical Center, Mahoning, Montour Co, PA
> Duncan, Irvin Wilfred
>> Death: Private

Germany
> ?
>> Birth: Private
> ?, Anna Margaret
>> Birth: Private
>> Marr: Private
> Dankert, ?
>> Birth: Private
> Geib, John Nicholas
>> Birth: Private
> Kepner, Eva Catherine
>> Birth: Private
> Kline, Henry
>> Birth: Private
>> Marr: Private
> Loyman, John Jacob
>> Birth: Private
>> Marr: Private
> Neipp, Anna Maria Catherine
>> Birth: Private

Germany (con't)
>> Marr: Private
> Oberlander, Peter
>> Birth: Private
>> Marr: Private
> Surr, Catherine
>> Birth: Private
>> Marr: Private

Hallowing Run, Northumberland Co, PA
> McCloud, Catherine
>> Birth: Private

Hanover, York Co, PA
> Baugher, Susan
>> Marr: Private
> Oberlander, Jacob
>> Marr: Private
> Warner, Maria Catherine
>> Birth: Private

Harrisburg, Dauphin Co, PA
> Layman, Mabel E
>> Death: Private

Hazleton State Hospital, Hazleton, Luzerne Co, PA
> Overlander, Rebecca Jane
>> Death: Private

Heidelberg, Lancaster (Lebanon) Co, PA
> Oberlander, Peter
>> Death: Private

Heidelberg, Lancaster Co, PA
> Oberlander, Peter
>> Prob: Private
>> Will: Private

Hellam, York Co, PA
> Geib, John Nicholas
>> Death: Private
>> Will: Private
>> Res: Private

Hempfield, Lancaster Co, PA
> Geib, John Nicholas
>> Res: Private
> Kline, Henry
>> Census: Private

Home, Sunbury, Northumberland Co, PA
> McCloud, Catherine
>> Death: Private

Howard Methodist Cemetery, Howard, Centre Co, PA
> Layman, Michael
>> Burial: Private
> Neal, Rachel

Howard Methodist Cemetery, Howard, Centre Co, PA (con't)

> Burial: Private

Howard Tp, Centre Co, PA

Layman, Michael
> Will: Private

Howard, Centre Co, PA

Layman, Michael
> Census: Private

Layman, Michael
> Death: Private

Neal, Rachel
> Death: Private

Howard, Centre Co, PA (Leyman)

Layman, Michael
> Census: Private

Howard, Centre Co, PA (Lyman)

Layman, Michael
> Census: Private
> Census: Private

Howard, Centre Co, PA (Lymon)

Layman, Michael
> Census: Private

Howard, Centre Co, PA (son John Layman)

Neal, Rachel
> Census: Private

Hummels Wharf Fire Co, Finanacial & recording Sec., Rescue Hose Co Sby.

Duncan, Irvin Wilfred
> Member: Private

husband

?, Elizabeth
> Census: Private
> Census: Private

?, Elizabeth
> Census: Private
> Census: Private
> Census: Private

?, Mary
> Census: Private
> Census: Private

Baugher, Susan
> Census: Private
> Census: Private

Kepner, Eva Catherine
> Census: Private

Klein, Sarah
> Census: Private
> Census: Private

Neal, Rachel
> Census: Private

husband (con't)
               Census: Private
               Census: Private
               Census: Private
   Surr, Catherine
               Census: Private
               Census: Private
               Census: Private
   Warner, Maria Catherine
               Census: Private
               Census: Private
               Census: Private

IL
   ?, Living
               Birth: Private

Ireland
   ?, Nancy
               Birth: Private

J. Hartman, Sunbury, Northumberland Co, PA
   Duncan, William
               Funeral: Private

Jac. Oberlander)
   ?, Elizabeth
               Census: Private

Jefferson, Codorus, York Co, PA
   Oberlander, Michael Baugher
               Birth: Private

JJ Sullivan
   Layman, Joseph Pierce
               Funeral: Private

Lancaster Co, PA
   ?, Anna Margaret
               Death: Private
               Prob: Private
   Kline, Henry
               Prob: Private
   Loyman, John Jacob
               Death: Private
   Neipp, Anna Maria Catherine
               Death: Private

Lower Augusta, Northumberland Co, PA
   ?, Mary
               Census: Private
               Census: Private
               Census: Private
               Census: Private
   McCloud, Catherine
               Census: Private
   McCloud, David

Lower Augusta, Northumberland Co, PA (con't)
        Census: Private
        Prob: Private

Lower Augusta, Northumberland Co, PA (Daniel Mcleod)
  McCloud, David
        Census: Private

Lower Chanceford, York Co, PA
  Layman, Joseph Pierce
        Census: Private
        Census: Private
  Layman, Michael
        Death: Private
        Census: Private
        Census: Private
        Census: Private
        Census: Private
  Raymond, Elmira Elizabeth
        Death: Private
        Census: Private
        Census: Private
        Census: Private
        Census: Private

M. Quay Olley [Olley-Gotlob] Funeral Home, 539 Race St., Sunbury, Northumberland Co, PA
  Duncan, Irvin Wilfred
        Funeral: Private

Manheim, York Co, PA
  ?, Judith
        Census: Private
  Werner, John George
        Census: Private

Manheim, York Co, PA (Overland)
  Oberlander, Jacob
        Census: Private

Manor Tp, Lancaster Co, PA
  Klein, Peter Michael?
        Death: Private
        Will: Private
        Prob: Private

Manor, Lancaster Co, PA
  Klein, Sarah
        Birth: Private
        Census: Private
  Kline, Henry
        Census: Private

Marietta, Lancaster Co, PA
  Layman, Michael
        Birth: Private

Maytown, York Co, PA

Maytown, York Co, PA (con't)
   Raymond, Elmira Elizabeth
         Birth: Private

Mifflin Co, PA
   Neal, Henry
         Census: Private

Mifflinburg, Northumberland (Union) Co, PA
   Layman, Michael
         Res: Private
   Neal, Henry
         Res: Private

Milesburg, Northumberland (Centre) Co, PA
   Layman, Michael
         Birth: Private

Monroe, Snyder Co, PA
   Anderson, Mary "Mamie" Lucetta
         Census: Private

Montour Co, PA
   Anderson, Mary "Mamie" Lucetta
         Prob: Private

Mountain Eagle, Centre Co, PA
   Layman, Michael
         Res: Private

NB
   ?, Living
         Birth: Private

Northumberland (Union) Co, PA
   Layman, Michael
         Res: Private
   Neal, Henry
         Death: Private
         Marr: Private

Northumberland Co, PA
   ?, Mary
         Death: Private
   Duncan, Frederick (Fritz Dankert)
         Death: Private
         Marr: Private
   McCloud, Catherine
         Marr: Private
   McCloud, David
         Death: Private

Northumberland?, PA
   ?, Mary
         Marr: Private
   Layman, Michael
         Marr: Private
   McCloud, David

Northumberland?, PA (con't)
>> Marr: Private

> Neal, Rachel
>> Marr: Private

Old Cemetery Sunbury, Northumberland Co, PA
> Duncan, Frederick (Fritz Dankert)
>> Burial: Private

Old Codorus, York Co, PA
> Miller, Andrew
>> Census: Private

Old Sunbury Cemetery, Sunbury, Northumberland Co, PA
> McCloud, Catherine
>> Burial: Private

P? Manor, Weatherly, Carbon, PA
> Overlander, Rebecca Jane
>> Funeral: Private

PA
> ?
>> Birth: Private

> ?
>> Birth: Private

> ?, Anna Margaret?
>> Death: Private

> ?, Catherine
>> Birth: Private

> ?, Elizabeth
>> Birth: Private

> ?, Elizabeth
>> Birth: Private

> ?, Elizabeth
>> Birth: Private

> ?, Elizabeth
>> Birth: Private

> ?, Frances
>> Birth: Private

> ?, Ida
>> Birth: Private

> ?, Leah
>> Birth: Private

> ?, Living
>> Birth: Private

> ?, Mary
>> Birth: Private

> ?, Mary Ann
>> Birth: Private

> ?, Nancy?
>> Birth: Private
>> Marr: Private

> Baugher, Anna
>> Birth: Private

Baugher, Barbara
                    Birth: Private
Baugher, Catherine
                    Birth: Private
Baugher, Mary
                    Birth: Private
Dietz, Anna Charlotte
                    Birth: Private
Dodge, Ezra J
                    Birth: Private
Dunlop?, Mary
                    Birth: Private
Frye, Mary E
                    Birth: Private
Fuhrman, Susan
                    Birth: Private
Gipe, Amos
                    Birth: Private
Gipe, Anna Catherine
                    Birth: Private
Gipe, Anna Margaret "Peggy"
                    Birth: Private
Gipe, Anna Maria
                    Birth: Private
Gipe, Catherine
                    Birth: Private
Gipe, Catherine Margaret
                    Birth: Private
Gipe, Daniel
                    Birth: Private
Gipe, Elizabeth
                    Birth: Private
Gipe, Eva
                    Birth: Private
Gipe, Jacob
                    Birth: Private
Gipe, Lena L
                    Birth: Private
Gipe, Lydia
                    Birth: Private
Gipe, Lydia
                    Birth: Private
Gipe, Margaret
                    Birth: Private
Gipe, Maria Elizabeth
                    Birth: Private
Gipe, Maria Magdalena "Polly"
                    Birth: Private
Gipe, Mary "Polly"
                    Birth: Private
Gipe, Michael

Birth: Private

Gipe, Nicholas

Birth: Private

Heffner, Sarah Amanda

Birth: Private

Kerstetter, James F

Birth: Private

Klein, Christian

Birth: Private

Layman, Catherine

Birth: Private

Layman, Charles Gibbs

Birth: Private

Layman, Chester A

Birth: Private

Layman, Christina

Birth: Private

Layman, Daniel Brunner

Birth: Private

Layman, David R

Birth: Private

Layman, Earl William

Birth: Private

Layman, Elizabeth

Birth: Private

Layman, Elizabeth

Birth: Private

Layman, Elmira "Ella"

Birth: Private

Layman, George

Birth: Private

Layman, Henry

Birth: Private

Layman, Henry

Birth: Private

Layman, Jacob

Birth: Private

Layman, Jacob L

Birth: Private

Layman, John

Birth: Private

Layman, Joseph P

Birth: Private

Layman, Lillian "Lillie" J

Birth: Private

Layman, Lillian "Lillie" May

Birth: Private

Layman, Living

Birth: Private

Layman, Living

Birth: Private

Layman, Living
> Birth: Private

Layman, Mabel E
> Birth: Private

Layman, Margaret Edna
> Birth: Private

Layman, Mary E
> Birth: Private

Layman, Rachel
> Birth: Private

Layman, Sarah
> Birth: Private

Layman, Sarah
> Birth: Private

Layman, Sophia M
> Birth: Private

Layman, Theodore A
> Birth: Private

Layman, Uriah
> Birth: Private

Lehman, Charles E
> Birth: Private

Masteller, Eula I
> Birth: Private

McCloud, Catherine
> Birth: Private

McCloud, Daniel
> Birth: Private

McCloud, David
> Birth: Private

McCloud, Frederick
> Birth: Private

McCloud, Jeremiah "Jerry"
> Birth: Private

McCloud, Joseph
> Birth: Private

McCloud, Judith
> Birth: Private

McCloud, Mary Ann
> Birth: Private

McCloud, Sarah
> Birth: Private

McCloud, William
> Birth: Private

McKinley, Margaret J
> Birth: Private

McNutt, William H
> Birth: Private

Medwick, Caroline "Carrie"
> Birth: Private

Miller, Salome "Sarah"

Birth: Private

Oberlander, Catherine
   Birth: Private

Oberlander, Catherine
   Birth: Private

Oberlander, Christian
   Birth: Private

Oberlander, Daniel
   Birth: Private

Oberlander, Daniel Baugher
   Birth: Private

Oberlander, Elizabeth
   Birth: Private

Oberlander, Elizabeth
   Birth: Private

Oberlander, Frederick
   Birth: Private

Oberlander, Jacob Baugher
   Birth: Private

Oberlander, John
   Birth: Private

Oberlander, Michael Baugher
   Birth: Private

Oberlander, Peter
   Birth: Private

Oberlander, Peter Baugher
   Birth: Private

Oberlander, Samuel
   Birth: Private

Oberlander, Samuel
   Birth: Private

Oberlander, Sarah Ann
   Birth: Private

Oberlander, Susan Warner
   Birth: Private

Oberlander, William
   Birth: Private

Oberlander, William
   Birth: Private

Overlander, Caroline
   Birth: Private

Overlander, Luther
   Birth: Private

Reed, Mary Salome
   Birth: Private

Reiman, John
   Marr: Private

Rexroth, Charles Wesley
   Birth: Private

Runkle, Jesse
   Birth: Private

PA (con't)

Strayer, Adam
> Birth: Private

Warner, Anna Maria
> Birth: Private

Warner, Catherine
> Birth: Private

Warner, Charles "Carl"
> Birth: Private

Warner, Elizabeth
> Birth: Private

Warner, Elizabeth
> Birth: Private

Warner, Eva
> Birth: Private

Warner, Henry
> Birth: Private

Warner, Henry
> Birth: Private

Warner, Jacob
> Birth: Private

Warner, Jacob
> Birth: Private

Warner, Jacob
> Birth: Private

Warner, John
> Birth: Private

Warner, John
> Birth: Private

Warner, Maria Catherine
> Birth: Private

Warner, Samuel
> Birth: Private

Warner, Samuel
> Birth: Private

Werner, John George
> Birth: Private

Workinger, Elizabeth
> Birth: Private

parents

Gipe, John
> Census: Private

Gipe, Sarah "Sallie" Ann
> Census: Private
> Census: Private

Klein, Sarah
> Census: Private
> Census: Private

Layman, Michael
> Census: Private
> Census: Private
> Census: Private

parents (con't)

Layman, Michael
        Census: Private
Layman, Michael
        Census: Private
Neal, Rachel
        Census: Private
Oberlander, Jacob
        Census: Private
Oberlander, Jacob Warner
        Census: Private
Raymond, Elmira Elizabeth
        Census: Private
        Census: Private

Peach Bottom, York Co, PA

Klein, Sarah
        Death: Private
        Census: Private
Layman, Michael
        Death: Private
Miller, Maria Elizabeth
        Census: Private
Warner, John Christian
        Census: Private

Peach Bottom, York Co, PA (Lyman)

Layman, Michael
        Census: Private

Philadelphia, PA

Layman, Michael
        Res: Private
Loyman, John Jacob
        Res: Private
Oberlander, Peter
        Res: Private

Philadelphia, Philadelphia, PA

Layman, Michael
        Birth: Private

Pomfret

Reed, Mary Salome
        Burial: Private

Pomfret Manor Cemetery, Sunbury, Northumberland Co, PA

Anderson, Mary "Mamie" Lucetta
        Burial: Private
Duncan, Irvin Wilfred
        Burial: Private
Duncan, William
        Burial: Private
Layman, Charlotte "Lottie" Virginia
        Burial: Private
Overlander, Rebecca Jane

Pomfret Manor Cemetery, Sunbury, Northumberland Co, PA (con't)
     Burial: Private

Potter Tp, Centre Co, PA
  Neal, Henry
     Res: Private

Prussia
  Dankert, ?
     Death: Private

Prussia (Germany)
  Duncan, Frederick (Fritz Dankert)
     Birth: Private

RD 2, Box 574, Danville, Mountour, PA 17821
  Anderson, Mary "Mamie" Lucetta
     Res: Private

RD 2, Selinsgrove, Snyder, PA 17870
  Duncan, Irvin Wilfred
     Res: Private

Relocated to York County
  Layman, Michael
     Res: Private

Republican
  Duncan, Irvin Wilfred
    PoliticalParty: Private

Safe Harbor, Conestoga, Lancaster Co, PA
  Kline, Henry
     Death: Private
     Res: Private
  Surr, Catherine
     Death: Private

Saint Lukes Evangelical Lutheran Cemetery, New Bridgeville, PA
  Oberlander, Michael Baugher
     Burial: Private
  Warner, Maria Catherine
     Burial: Private

Short St., Sunbury, Northumberland Co, PA
  Duncan, Frederick (Fritz Dankert)
     Res: Private

Shrewsburg, York Co, PA
  Oberlander, Jacob
     Census: Private

Simmern, Rhineland-Palatinate, Germany
  Bager, John George William
     Birth: Private

son Jacob
  Miller, Maria Elizabeth
     Census: Private

South ward York, York Co, PA
   ?, Elizabeth
         Census: Private

St. Jacobs (Stone) Union, Glenville, York Co, PA
   Miller, Maria Elizabeth
         Baptism: Private
   Warner, John Christian
         Baptism: Private
   Warner, Maria Catherine
         Baptism: Private
   Werner, John George
         Burial: Private

St. Lukes (Stahleys) Lutheran, New Bridgeville, York Co, PA
   Gipe, Sarah "Sallie" Ann
         Burial: Private
         Marr: Private
   Oberlander, Jacob Warner
         Marr: Private

St. Matthews Lutheran, Hanover, York Co, PA
   Oberlander, Jacob
         Baptism: Private
   Oberlander, Michael Baugher
         Baptism: Private

St. Michael's Zion Lutheran Church, Philadelphia, Philadelphia, PA
   Layman, Michael
         Baptism: Private

Sunbury, Northumberland Co, PA
   Anderson, Mary "Mamie" Lucetta
         Census: Private
         Res: Private
         Marr: Private
   Duncan, Charles "Charley"
         Birth: Private
         Death: Private
   Duncan, Frederick (Fritz Dankert)
         Census: Private
         Census: Private
   Duncan, Gertrude "Gerty"
         Birth: Private
   Duncan, Hannah Artila "Lilly"
         Birth: Private
   Duncan, Irvin Wilfred
         Birth: Private
         Census: Private
         Census: Private
         Res: Private
         Marr: Private
   Duncan, Melinda E
         Birth: Private
         Death: Private

Sunbury, Northumberland Co, PA (con't)

Duncan, Sarah "Sallie"
> Birth: Private
> Death: Private

Duncan, William
> Birth: Private
> Birth: Private
> Death: Private
> Census: Private
> Census: Private
> Res: Private
> Will: Private
> Prob: Private
> Marr: Private

Frye, Mary E
> Marr: Private

Layman, Charlotte "Lottie" Virginia
> Census: Private
> Census: Private
> Res: Private
> Marr: Private

Layman, Living
> Birth: Private

McCloud, Catherine
> Census: Private
> Census: Private

McCloud, Jeremiah "Jerry"
> Marr: Private

Overlander, Rebecca Jane
> Census: Private

Sunbury, Northumberland Co, PA (Laymer)

Overlander, Rebecca Jane
> Census: Private

Sunbury, Northumberland Co, PA (Laynon)

Layman, Joseph Pierce
> Census: Private

Sunbury, Northumberland Co, PA (Mary)

McCloud, Catherine
> Census: Private

Sunbury, Northumberland Co, PA (Willard)

Layman, Charlotte "Lottie" Virginia
> Census: Private
> Census: Private

Sunbury, Northumberland Co., PA

McCloud, Daniel
> Death: Private

Reed, Mary Salome
> Death: Private

Susquehanna Ave., Sunbury, Northumberland Co, PA

Duncan, Irvin Wilfred

Susquehanna Ave., Sunbury, Northumberland Co, PA (con't)
> Res: Private

Trinity Lutheran, New Holland, Lancaster Co, PA
Klein, Sarah
> Marr: Private

Layman, Michael
> Marr: Private

Upper Chanceford, York Co, PA
Gipe, Jacob
> Census: Private

Gipe, John
> Census: Private

Miller, Maria Elizabeth
> Census: Private

Oberlander, Michael Baugher
> Census: Private

Warner, John Christian
> Census: Private

Upper Chanceford, York Co, PA (Geise)
Gipe, Jacob
> Census: Private

Upper Chanceford, York Co, PA (Giese)
Gipe, John
> Census: Private

VL Seebold, 601 N High St, Selinsgrove, Snyder Co, PA
Anderson, Mary "Mamie" Lucetta
> Funeral: Private

Weatherly, Carbon, PA
Overlander, Rebecca Jane
> Res: Private

West Buffalo, Northumberland (Union) Co, PA
Layman, Michael
> Res: Private

Neal, Henry
> Census: Private

West Hempfield, Lancaster Co, PA
Kline, Henry
> Census: Private

West Manchester, York Co, PA
Reiman, John
> Census: Private

Windsor, York Co, PA
Gipe, Jacob
> Res: Private

York (Adams) Co, PA
Baugher, Christina
> Birth: Private

York (Adams) Co, PA (con't)

    Baugher, Elizabeth
                Birth: Private
    Baugher, William
                Birth: Private

York Co, PA

    ?, Elizabeth
                Death: Private
                Marr: Private
    ?, Elizabeth
                Death: Private
                Marr: Private
    ?, Judith
                Census: Private
    Bager, John George William
                Census: Private
    Dietz, Anna Charlotte
                Death: Private
    Gipe, Henry
                Birth: Private
    Gipe, Jacob
                Birth: Private
                Census: Private
                Marr: Private
    Gipe, John
                Birth: Private
                Marr: Private
    Gipe, Peter
                Birth: Private
    Hamm, Anna Maria
                Birth: Private
                Death: Private
                Baptism: Private
                Marr: Private
    Miller, Andrew
                Birth: Private
                Marr: Private
    Miller, Anna Christina
                Birth: Private
    Miller, Catherine
                Birth: Private
    Miller, David
                Birth: Private
    Miller, John
                Birth: Private
    Miller, Margaret
                Birth: Private
    Miller, Maria Elizabeth
                Death: Private
                Marr: Private
    Miller, Maria Magdalena "Molly"
                Birth: Private

York Co, PA (con't)

Oberlander, Mary Jane
        Birth: Private

Overlander, Adeline
        Birth: Private

Overlander, Barbara Alice
        Birth: Private

Overlander, Edward
        Birth: Private

Overlander, Emaline Ellen
        Birth: Private

Overlander, Jacob L
        Birth: Private

Overlander, Margaret "Maggie" Jane
        Birth: Private

Overlander, Samuel Washington
        Birth: Private

Overlander, Sarah Catherine
        Birth: Private

Reiman, John
        Death: Private
        Census: Private

Rohrbach, David
        Birth: Private

Tome, Peter
        Birth: Private

Warner, John Christian
        Birth: Private
        Death: Private
        Marr: Private

Werner, John George
        Census: Private

York, York Co, PA

Dietz, Anna Charlotte
        Marr: Private

Geib, John Nicholas
        Marr: Private

Reiman, John
        Will: Private

York?, PA

?, Judith
        Marr: Private

Bager, John George William
        Marr: Private

Kepner, Eva Catherine
        Marr: Private

Werner, John George
        Marr: Private

Zion Evangelical Lutheran Church, Sunbury, Northumberland Co, PA

Duncan, William
        Baptism: Private

Chapter Four

Our family's kinship.

How we are all related to one another from present to distant past and the descendants of Frederick Duncan.

Kinship

Name:	Birth Date:	Relationship:
?		Husband of aunt
?		2nd great grandfather
?		2nd great grandmother
?	Abt. 1810	Great grandmother
?, Anna Catherine	Abt. 1730	Wife of 4th great grandfather
?, Anna Elizabeth		Wife of 4th great grandfather
?, Anna Margaret	Abt. 1740	4th great grandmother
?, Anna Margaret?	Abt. 1740	4th great grandmother
?, Barbara	Abt. 1760	Wife of 3rd great grand uncle
?, Catherine		Wife of 4th great grand uncle
?, Catherine	1808	Wife of 2nd great grand uncle
?, Elizabeth	Abt. 1762	3rd great grandmother
?, Elizabeth	1795	2nd great grandmother
?, Elizabeth	1796	Wife of 2nd great grand uncle
?, Elizabeth	1810	Wife of 2nd great grand uncle
?, Elizabeth	1816	Wife of 2nd great grand uncle
?, Frances	1888	Wife of uncle
?, Living		Wife of uncle
?, Ida	1887	Wife of uncle
?, Isabelle	1840	Wife of 1st great grand uncle
?, Judith	March 1746	4th great grandmother
?, Leah	1811	Wife of 2nd great grand uncle
?, Mary	Abt. 1815	Great grandmother
?, Mary	1860	Step grandmother
?, Mary Ann	1840	Wife of grand uncle
?, Living		Wife of uncle
?, Nancy	1815	Wife of 2nd great grand uncle
?, Nancy?	Abt. 1790	2nd great grandmother
?, Living		Wife of uncle
?, Sarah		Step grandmother
?, Temperance	1790	Wife of 3rd great grandfather
Albright, Elizabeth	1810	Wife of 2nd great grand uncle
Anderson, Mary "Mamie" Lucetta	April 11, 1908	Wife
Bager, John George William	April 15, 1750	4th great grandfather
Baugher, Anna	1788	3rd great grand aunt
Baugher, Barbara	Abt. 1780	3rd great grand aunt
Baugher, Catherine	Abt. 1780	3rd great grand aunt
Baugher, Catherine Margaret		4th great grand aunt

Name:	Birth Date:	Relationship:
Baugher, Christina	1786	3rd great grand aunt
Baugher, Elizabeth	1775	3rd great grand aunt
Baugher, John Frederick	1754	4th great grand uncle
Baugher, Mary	Abt. 1780	3rd great grand aunt
Baugher, Samuel?		4th great grand uncle
Baugher, Susan	1773	3rd great grandmother
Baugher, William	1784	3rd great grand uncle
Baymiller, Frederick	Abt. 1780	Husband of 2nd great grand aunt
Bell, Mary Elizabeth	1840	Wife of grand uncle
Bowman, Catherine	1810	Wife of 2nd great grand uncle
Cramer, Catherine Elizabeth	Abt. 1790	Wife of 3rd great grand uncle
Cramer, Julia	Abt. 1790	Wife of 3rd great grand uncle
Dankert, ?	Abt. 1810	Great grandfather
Dietz, Anna Charlotte	1733	4th great grandmother
Ditty, Peter		Husband of 3rd great grand aunt
Dodge, Ezra J	Abt. 1891	Husband of aunt
Duncan, Charles "Charley"	June 26, 1882	Uncle
Duncan, Frederick (Fritz Dankert)	Abt. 1839	Paternal grandfather
Duncan, Gertrude "Gerty"	October 12, 1878	Aunt
Duncan, Hannah Artila "Lilly"	December 02, 1880	Aunt
Duncan, Irvin Wilfred	November 27, 1901	Self
Duncan, Melinda E	January 17, 1871	Aunt
Duncan, Sarah "Sallie"	March 14, 1872	Aunt
Duncan, William	January 16, 1876	Father
Dunlop?, Mary	1846	Wife of 1st great grand uncle
Dustin, James		Husband of 3rd great grand aunt
Frye, Mary E	1871	Wife of grand uncle
Fuhrman, Susan	1802	Wife of 2nd great grand uncle
Geib, John Nicholas	1730	4th great grandfather
Geiser, Albert	1870	Husband of aunt
Gipe, Amos	1835	Great grand uncle
Gipe, Anna Catherine	1765	3rd great grand aunt
Gipe, Anna Margaret "Peggy"	1787	2nd great grand aunt
Gipe, Anna Maria	Abt. 1780	3rd great grand aunt
Gipe, Catherine	1785	2nd great grand aunt
Gipe, Catherine Margaret	1826	Great grand aunt
Gipe, Daniel	Abt. 1797	2nd great grand uncle
Gipe, Elizabeth		Great grand aunt
Gipe, Eva	Abt. 1770	3rd great grand aunt
Gipe, Henry	1756	3rd great grand uncle

Name:	Birth Date:	Relationship:
Gipe, Jacob	Abt. 1761	3rd great grandfather
Gipe, Jacob	1793	2nd great grand uncle
Gipe, John	October 17, 1790	2nd great grandfather
Gipe, Lena L	Abt. 1834	Great grand aunt
Gipe, Lydia	1801	2nd great grand aunt
Gipe, Lydia	1837	Great grand aunt
Gipe, Margaret	Abt. 1770	3rd great grand aunt
Gipe, Maria Elizabeth	Abt. 1781	3rd great grand aunt
Gipe, Maria Magdalena "Polly"	1795	2nd great grand aunt
Gipe, Mary "Polly"	1824	Great grand aunt
Gipe, Michael	1828	Great grand uncle
Gipe, Nicholas	Abt. 1770	3rd great grand uncle
Gipe, Peter	1755	3rd great grand uncle
Gipe, Sarah "Sallie" Ann	1834	Great grandmother
Gorrence, John		Husband of 3rd great grand aunt
Grokes, Anna Catherine	1751	Wife of 4th great grandfather
Hahn, Solomon		Husband of 3rd great grand aunt
Hamm, Anna Maria	November 10, 1763	4th great grandmother
Hamm, Christina?		4th great grand aunt
Hamm, John?		4th great grand uncle
Hamm, Peter		4th great grand uncle
Heffner, Sarah Amanda	1871	Wife of grand uncle
Hess, Phoebe A	1870	Wife of grand uncle
Hivner, John	Abt. 1790	Husband of 2nd great grand aunt
Ilges, Wesley J	1850	Husband of grand aunt
Kepner, Eva Catherine	June 09, 1753	4th great grandmother
Kerstetter, James F	October 1881	Husband of aunt
King, Michael	Abt. 1760	Husband of 3rd great grand aunt
Klein, ?	Abt. 1790	2nd great grand uncle
Klein, Christian	1788	2nd great grand uncle
Klein, Elizabeth	Abt. 1790	2nd great grand aunt
Klein, Peter	Abt. 1790	2nd great grand uncle
Klein, Peter Michael?	Abt. 1740	4th great grandfather
Klein, Sarah	1796	2nd great grandmother
Klein, Susan	Abt. 1790	2nd great grand aunt
Kline, Christopher?	Abt. 1774	3rd great grand uncle
Kline, Henry	Abt. 1770	3rd great grandfather
Kline, Jacob?	Abt. 1772	3rd great grand uncle
Kline, Peter		Husband of 3rd great grand aunt
Kline, Peter?	Abt. 1768	3rd great grand uncle

Name:	Birth Date:	Relationship:
Lantz, Anna Catherine	Abt. 1760	Wife of 3rd great grand uncle
Layman, Abraham		3rd great grand uncle
Layman, Catherine	Abt. 1825	Great grand aunt
Layman, Charles Gibbs	1859	Grand uncle
Layman, Charlotte "Lottie" Virginia	May 12, 1879	Mother
Layman, Chester A	August 1885	Uncle
Layman, Christina	Abt. 1825	Great grand aunt
Layman, Daniel		3rd great grand uncle
Layman, Daniel Brunner	1884	Uncle
Layman, David R	1841	Great grand uncle
Layman, Earl William	Abt. 1880	Uncle
Layman, Elizabeth		3rd great grand aunt
Layman, Elizabeth		2nd great grand aunt
Layman, Elizabeth	Abt. 1825	Great grand aunt
Layman, Elmira "Ella"	1853	Grand aunt
Layman, George	Abt. 1825	Great grand uncle
Layman, Henry		3rd great grand uncle
Layman, Henry		2nd great grand uncle
Layman, Henry	1834	Great grand uncle
Layman, Jacob		3rd great grand uncle
Layman, Jacob		2nd great grand uncle
Layman, Jacob L	1846	Grand uncle
Layman, John		3rd great grand uncle
Layman, John	1812	2nd great grand uncle
Layman, Joseph P	1887	Uncle
Layman, Joseph Pierce	January 08, 1859	Maternal grandfather
Layman, Living		Uncle
Layman, Lillian "Lillie" J	1860	Grand aunt
Layman, Lillian "Lillie" May	1878	Aunt
Layman, Mabel E	May 18, 1892	Aunt
Layman, Margaret Edna	1893	Aunt
Layman, Living		Aunt
Layman, Mary E	1849	Grand aunt
Layman, Michael	December 11, 1764	3rd great grandfather
Layman, Michael	Abt. 1795	2nd great grandfather
Layman, Michael	October 10, 1818	Great grandfather
Layman, Living		Uncle
Layman, Rachel		2nd great grand aunt
Layman, Living		Uncle
Layman, Sarah		2nd great grand aunt

Name:	Birth Date:	Relationship:
Layman, Sarah	1847	Grand aunt
Layman, Sophia M	1834	Great grand aunt
Layman, Theodore A	1862	Grand uncle
Layman, Theodore Augusta	August 1886	Uncle
Layman, Uriah	1848	Grand uncle
Lehman, Charles E	1883	Uncle
Loyman, John Jacob	Abt. 1740	4th great grandfather
Masteller, Eula I	1892	Wife of uncle
Mattere, Anna Catherine		Wife of 4th great grand uncle
McCleary, Harriet "Hattie"	1850	Wife of grand uncle
McCloud, Catherine	January 1847	Paternal grandmother
McCloud, Daniel	1849	Grand uncle
McCloud, David	Abt. 1807	Great grandfather
McCloud, Frederick	1852	Grand uncle
McCloud, Jeremiah "Jerry"	1853	Grand uncle
McCloud, John?	Abt. 1780	2nd great grandfather
McCloud, Joseph	1836	Grand uncle
McCloud, Judith	1855	Grand aunt
McCloud, Mary Ann	1844	Grand aunt
McCloud, Sarah	1839	Grand aunt
McCloud, William	1856	Grand uncle
McKinley, Margaret J	1859	Wife of grand uncle
McNutt, William H	Abt. 1887	Stepfather
Medwick, Caroline "Carrie"	1859	Wife of grand uncle
Medwick, Casper	1850	Husband of grand aunt
Miller, Andrew	March 14, 1752	4th great grandfather
Miller, Anna Christina	1784	3rd great grand aunt
Miller, Barbara	1772	4th great grand aunt
Miller, Catherine	1779	3rd great grand aunt
Miller, David	1795	3rd great grand uncle
Miller, Jacob	1765	4th great grand uncle
Miller, John	1790	3rd great grand uncle
Miller, Margaret	1782	3rd great grand aunt
Miller, Maria Elizabeth	1768	4th great grand aunt
Miller, Maria Elizabeth	October 17, 1777	3rd great grandmother
Miller, Maria Magdalena "Molly"	1788	3rd great grand aunt
Miller, Michael	1770	4th great grand uncle
Miller, Salome "Sarah"	1793	3rd great grand aunt
Myers, Dorothy		Wife of uncle
Myers, Tempest Valentine		Husband of grand aunt
Neal, ?		3rd great grand uncle

Name:	Birth Date:	Relationship:
Neal, ?		3rd great grand aunt
Neal, Henry	Abt. 1740	4th great grandfather
Neal, Rachel	December 04, 1765	3rd great grandmother
Neipp, Anna Maria Catherine	1749	4th great grandmother
Oberlander, Catherine		Great grand aunt
Oberlander, Catherine	1806	2nd great grand aunt
Oberlander, Christian	1838	Great grand uncle
Oberlander, Daniel	1811	2nd great grand uncle
Oberlander, Daniel Baugher		Great grand uncle
Oberlander, Elizabeth	1807	2nd great grand aunt
Oberlander, Elizabeth	1823	Great grand aunt
Oberlander, Frederick	1814	2nd great grand uncle
Oberlander, Jacob	1768	3rd great grandfather
Oberlander, Jacob Baugher	1803	2nd great grand uncle
Oberlander, Jacob Warner	1819	Great grandfather
Oberlander, John	1801	2nd great grand uncle
Oberlander, Mary Jane	1830	Great grand aunt
Oberlander, Michael Baugher	February 23, 1798	2nd great grandfather
Oberlander, Michael Baugher	1835	Great grand uncle
Oberlander, Peter	January 01, 1745	4th great grandfather
Oberlander, Peter	1799	2nd great grand uncle
Oberlander, Peter Baugher		Great grand uncle
Oberlander, Samuel		Great grand uncle
Oberlander, Samuel	1812	2nd great grand uncle
Oberlander, Sarah Ann		Great grand aunt
Oberlander, Susan Warner	1833	Great grand aunt
Oberlander, William	1802	2nd great grand uncle
Oberlander, William	1833	Great grand uncle
Overlander, Adeline	1858	Grand aunt
Overlander, Barbara Alice	1868	Grand aunt
Overlander, Caroline	1861	Grand aunt
Overlander, Edward	1857	Grand uncle
Overlander, Emaline Ellen	1866	Grand aunt
Overlander, Jacob L	1869	Grand uncle
Overlander, Luther	1855	Grand uncle
Overlander, Margaret "Maggie" Jane	1864	Grand aunt
Overlander, Rebecca Jane	October 1859	Maternal grandmother
Overlander, Samuel Washington	1862	Grand uncle
Overlander, Sarah Catherine	1855	Grand aunt
Raymond, Elmira Elizabeth	January 17, 1824	Great grandmother

Name:	Birth Date:	Relationship:
Reed, Mary Salome	1850	Wife of grand uncle
Regal, Jacob		Husband of 3rd great grand aunt
Reiman, John	Abt. 1790	2nd great grandfather
Rexroth, Charles Wesley	1859	Husband of grand aunt
Rexroth, Samuel David	1860	Husband of grand aunt
Rohrbach, David	1789	Husband of 3rd great grand aunt
Rohrbach, Henry	1778	Husband of 3rd great grand aunt
Runkle, Jesse	1821	Husband of 1st great grand aunt
Schreiber, ?		Husband of 4th great grandmother
Schuler, Living		Wife of uncle
Smith, John	1820	Husband of 1st great grand aunt
Strayer, Adam	1794	Husband of 2nd great grand aunt
Surr, Catherine	Abt. 1770	3rd great grandmother
Tome, Peter	1825	Husband of 1st great grand aunt
Warner, Adam?		4th great grand uncle
Warner, Anna Maria	1790	3rd great grand aunt
Warner, Catherine	1778	3rd great grand aunt
Warner, Charles "Carl"	Abt. 1772	3rd great grand uncle
Warner, Charles?		4th great grand uncle
Warner, Elizabeth	1784	3rd great grand aunt
Warner, Elizabeth	1805	2nd great grand aunt
Warner, Eva	1812	2nd great grand aunt
Warner, Henry	Abt. 1772	3rd great grand uncle
Warner, Henry	1805	2nd great grand uncle
Warner, Jacob	1782	3rd great grand uncle
Warner, Jacob	1786	3rd great grand uncle
Warner, Jacob	1803	2nd great grand uncle
Warner, John	1771	3rd great grand uncle
Warner, John	1815	2nd great grand uncle
Warner, John Christian	October 24, 1775	3rd great grandfather
Warner, Maria Catherine	1791	3rd great grand aunt
Warner, Maria Catherine	March 21, 1798	2nd great grandmother
Warner, Melchior?		4th great grand uncle
Warner, Samuel	1800	2nd great grand uncle
Warner, Samuel	1815	2nd great grand uncle
Wehrly, Samuel		Husband of 3rd great grand aunt
Werner, John George	February 23, 1754	4th great grandfather
Willard, William Grant	1874	Stepfather
Wise, John	1800	Husband of 2nd great grand aunt
Workinger, Elizabeth	1814	Wife of 2nd great grand uncle

Name:	Birth Date:	Relationship:
Wright, William	1850	Husband of grand aunt

Descendants of Frederick Duncan

1 Frederick (Fritz Dankert) Duncan b: Abt. 1839 in Prussia (Germany), d: 1882 in Northumberland Co, PA

... + Catherine McCloud b: January 1847 in Hallowing Run, Northumberland Co, PA, m: Abt. 1870 in Northumberland Co, PA, d: January 02, 1903 in Home, Sunbury, Northumberland Co, PA

......2 Melinda E Duncan b: January 17, 1871 in Sunbury, Northumberland Co, PA, d: April 27, 1933 in Sunbury, Northumberland Co, PA

...... + Albert Geiser b: 1870, d: 1948

.........3 Elsie Catherine Geiser b: 1893 in PA, d: 1985

.... + Harry Conrad Culp b: 1892 in PA

............4 David Albert Culp b: 1919 in PA, d: 1996

............4 Harry Conrad Culp b: 1924 in PA, d: 1995

............4 Robert Leroy Culp b: 1925 in PA, d: 1945

.........3 Carrie E Geiser b: 1894 in PA, d: 1983

.........3 Georgetta Geiser b: 1895 in PA, d: 1991

.... + Howard Elmer Eister b: 1895 in PA, d: 1975

.........3 Living Geiser

.... + Living ?

............4 Gordon A Geiser b: 1925 in PA, d: 2005

......2 Sarah "Sallie" Duncan b: March 14, 1872 in Sunbury, Northumberland Co, PA, d: February 03, 1915 in Sunbury, Northumberland Co, PA

...... + ?

.........3 Harry "Red" Leroy Duncan b: June 19, 1896 in Sunbury, Northumberland Co, PA, d: April 23, 1956 in Sunbury, Northumberland Co, PA

.... + Living Herrold

............4 Living Duncan

............4 Living Duncan

......2 William Duncan b: January 16, 1876 in Sunbury, Northumberland Co, PA, d: September 11, 1906 in Sunbury, Northumberland Co, PA

...... + Charlotte "Lottie" Virginia Layman b: May 12, 1879 in Brogueville, York Co, PA, m: April 13, 1899 in Sunbury, Northumberland Co, PA, d: February 29, 1936 in at Irvin's home, Monroe, Snyder Co, PA

.........3 Irvin Wilfred Duncan b: November 27, 1901 in Sunbury, Northumberland Co, PA, d: April 08, 1978 in Geisinger Medical Center, Mahoning, Montour Co, PA

.... + Mary "Mamie" Lucetta Anderson b: April 11, 1908 in At home, Sunbury, Northumberland Co, PA, m: June 07, 1926 in Sunbury, Northumberland Co, PA, d: April 03, 1989 in Derry, Montour Co, PA

............4 Charlotte E Duncan b: December 04, 1926 in PA, d: 1926

............4 Ethel L Duncan b: December 04, 1926 in PA, d: 2011

.... + Living Cameron

...............5 Living Cameron

...............5 Living Cameron

.... + Patricia ?

.... + Debra ?

...............5 Living Cameron

.... + Richard Smith

...............5 Living Cameron

.... + Michael Hampton

.... + James Wolfe

............4 Living Duncan

.... + Living Newberry
.............5 Living Duncan
.... + Ann Philips
.............5 Living Duncan
.... + Gene Gormley
.............5 Living Duncan
.... + Jeffrey Davis
.... + Dominick Silla
.... + Manfred Klatt
.... + Living James
.... + Living ?
...........4 Living Duncan
.... + Living Zeigler
.............5 Living Zeigler
.... + Kathy Loeffler
.............5 Living Zeigler
.... + L Williams
.............5 Living Zeigler
.... + D A Clark
.............5 Living Zeigler
.... + J Renard
...........4 Ralph Richard Duncan b: 1934 in PA, d: 1934
...........4 Living Duncan
.... + Living Thompson
.............5 Living St. Thompson
.... + Living ?
.............5 Living Thompson
.... + Living ?
.............5 Living Thompson
.... + Melvalean Curry b: January 15, 1967 in Jefferson, Philadelphia Co, PA, d: May 28, 2008 in
             Boynton Beach, Palm Beach, Florida, USA
.... + Living Wittle
.... + Living Romano
...........4 Living Duncan
.... + Living Drendall
.............5 Living Duncan
.... + A ?
......2 Gertrude "Gerty" Duncan b: October 12, 1878 in Sunbury, Northumberland Co, PA
......2 Hannah Artila "Lilly" Duncan b: December 02, 1880 in Sunbury, Northumberland Co, PA, d: Aft.
      1930
...... + James F Kerstetter b: October 1881 in PA, d: Aft. 1930
.........3 Living Kerstetter
.... + Living ?
...........4 Living Kerstetter
...........4 Living Kerstetter
......2 Charles "Charley" Duncan b: June 26, 1882 in Sunbury, Northumberland Co, PA, d: February 12,
      1924 in Sunbury, Northumberland Co, PA
...... + Eula I Masteller b: 1892 in PA, m: 1909, d: Aft. 1930 in CA
.........3 Lillian K Duncan b: 1910 in PA, d: 1996 in CA
.... + Living Woods
.........3 Violet Loraine Duncan b: 1919 in PA, d: 1993 in CA
.... + ? Page
...........4 Larry Webster Page b: Abt. 1940, d: 2004

............4 Living Page
... + Sarah ?

Chapter Five

Our family's calendar.

Important annual dates of birth, marriage and death.

January 2014

January 2014
S M T W T F S
1 2 3 4
5 6 7 8 9 10 11
12 13 14 15 16 17 18
19 20 21 22 23 24 25
26 27 28 29 30 31

February 2014
S M T W T F S
1
2 3 4 5 6 7 8
9 10 11 12 13 14 15
16 17 18 19 20 21 22
23 24 25 26 27 28

Sunday	Monday	Tuesday	Wednesday	Thursday	Friday	Saturday
			1 Peter Oberlander	2 Catherine McCloud Duncan	3	4
5 Michael Layman	6	7	8 Joseph P. Layman	9	10	11
12 Judith ? Werner	13	14	15	16 William Duncan	17 Melinda E. Duncan Geiser Elmira E. Raymond Layman	18
19	20	21	22	23	24	25
26	27	28	29	30	31	

February 2014

February 2014
S M T W T F S
                1
2 3 4 5 6 7 8
9 10 11 12 13 14 15
16 17 18 19 20 21 22
23 24 25 26 27 28

March 2014
S M T W T F S
                1
2 3 4 5 6 7 8
9 10 11 12 13 14 15
16 17 18 19 20 21 22
23 24 25 26 27 28 29
30 31

Sunday	Monday	Tuesday	Wednesday	Thursday	Friday	Saturday
						1
2	3 Sarah ". Duncan ?	4	5	6 John J. Loyman	7	8
9	10	11	12 Charles ". Duncan	13	14	15
16	17	18	19	20 Joseph P. Layman	21	22
23 Michael B. Oberlander John G. Werner	24	25	26	27	28 (Feb 29) Charlotte ".V. Layman Duncan	

March 2014

March 2014
S M T W T F S
1
2 3 4 5 6 7 8
9 10 11 12 13 14 15
16 17 18 19 20 21 22
23 24 25 26 27 28 29
30 31

April 2014
S M T W T F S
1 2 3 4 5
6 7 8 9 10 11 12
13 14 15 16 17 18 19
20 21 22 23 24 25 26
27 28 29 30

Sunday	Monday	Tuesday	Wednesday	Thursday	Friday	Saturday
2	3	4	5	6	7	8
9	10	11 Eva C. Kepner Bager	12	13	14 Sarah ". Duncan ? Andrew Miller	1.
16	17	18	19	20	21 Maria C. Warner Oberlander	2:
23	24	25	26	27	28	2'
30	31					

April 2014

April 2014						
S	M	T	W	T	F	S
		1	2	3	4	5
6	7	8	9	10	11	12
13	14	15	16	17	18	19
20	21	22	23	24	25	26
27	28	29	30			

May 2014						
S	M	T	W	T	F	S
				1	2	3
4	5	6	7	8	9	10
11	12	13	14	15	16	17
18	19	20	21	22	23	24
25	26	27	28	29	30	31

Sunday	Monday	Tuesday	Wednesday	Thursday	Friday	Saturday
		1 Anna M.C. Neipp Oberlander	2	3 Mary ".L. Anderson Duncan Elmira E. and Michael Layman	4	5
6	7	8 Irvin W. Duncan	9	10	11 Mary ".L. Anderson Duncan	12 Jacob Oberlander
13 Charlotte ".V. and William Duncan	14	15 John G.W. Bager	16	17	18	19
20	21 Susan Baugher Oberlander	22	23	24	25	26
27 Melinda E. Duncan Geiser	28	29	30			

May 2014

May 2014
S M T W T F S
1 2 3
4 5 6 7 8 9 10
11 12 13 14 15 16 17
18 19 20 21 22 23 24
25 26 27 28 29 30 31

June 2014
S M T W T F S
1 2 3 4 5 6 7
8 9 10 11 12 13 14
15 16 17 18 19 20 21
22 23 24 25 26 27 28
29 30

Sunday	Monday	Tuesday	Wednesday	Thursday	Friday	Saturday
				1	2	3
4	5	6	7	8	9	10
11	12 Charlotte ".V. Layman Duncan	13	14	15	16	17 John G.W. Bager Michael Layman
18 Mabel E. Layman Dodge	19 David McCloud	20	21	22	23	24
25	26	27	28	29	30	31

June 2014

June 2014

S M T W T F S
1 2 3 4 5 6 7
8 9 10 11 12 13 14
15 16 17 18 19 20 21
22 23 24 25 26 27 28
29 30

July 2014

S M T W T F S
1 2 3 4 5
6 7 8 9 10 11 12
13 14 15 16 17 18 19
20 21 22 23 24 25 26
27 28 29 30 31

Sunday	Monday	Tuesday	Wednesday	Thursday	Friday	Saturday
1	2	3	4	5	6	7 Mary ".L. and Irvin W. Duncan
8	9 Eva C. Kepner Bager	10	11	12	13	14
15	16	17	18	19	20	21
22 nna M. Hamm Mille	23	24	25	26 Charles ". Duncan	27	28 Sarah and Michael Layman
29	30					

July 2014

July 2014

S	M	T	W	T	F	S
		1	2	3	4	5
6	7	8	9	10	11	12
13	14	15	16	17	18	19
20	21	22	23	24	25	26
27	28	29	30	31		

August 2014

S	M	T	W	T	F	S
					1	2
3	4	5	6	7	8	9
10	11	12	13	14	15	16
17	18	19	20	21	22	23
24	25	26	27	28	29	30
31						

Sunday	Monday	Tuesday	Wednesday	Thursday	Friday	Saturday
		1	2	3 Mary S. Reed McCloud	4	5
6	7	8	9	10	11	12
13	14	15	16	17	18	19
20	21	22	23	24	25	26
27	28	29 Daniel McCloud	30	31		

August 2014

August 2014

S	M	T	W	T	F	S
					1	2
3	4	5	6	7	8	9
10	11	12	13	14	15	16
17	18	19	20	21	22	23
24	25	26	27	28	29	30
31						

September 2014

S	M	T	W	T	F	S
	1	2	3	4	5	6
7	8	9	10	11	12	13
14	15	16	17	18	19	20
21	22	23	24	25	26	27
28	29	30				

Sunday	Monday	Tuesday	Wednesday	Thursday	Friday	Saturday
					1	2
3	4	5	6	7	8	9
10	11	12	13	14	15	16 John G. Werner
17 Maria C. and Michael B. Oberlander	18	19	20	21	22	23
24	25	26	27	28	29	30
31						

September 2014

September 2014

S	M	T	W	T	F	S
	1	2	3	4	5	6
7	8	9	10	11	12	13
14	15	16	17	18	19	20
21	22	23	24	25	26	27
28	29	30				

October 2014

S	M	T	W	T	F	S
			1	2	3	4
5	6	7	8	9	10	11
12	13	14	15	16	17	18
19	20	21	22	23	24	25
26	27	28	29	30	31	

Sunday	Monday	Tuesday	Wednesday	Thursday	Friday	Saturday
	1	2	3	4	5	6
7	8	9	10	11 William Duncan	12	13
14	15	16	17	18	19	20
21	22	23	24	25	26	27
28	29	30				

October 2014

October 2014

S	M	T	W	T	F	S
			1	2	3	4
5	6	7	8	9	10	11
12	13	14	15	16	17	18
19	20	21	22	23	24	25
26	27	28	29	30	31	

November 2014

S	M	T	W	T	F	S
						1
2	3	4	5	6	7	8
9	10	11	12	13	14	15
16	17	18	19	20	21	22
23	24	25	26	27	28	29
30						

Sunday	Monday	Tuesday	Wednesday	Thursday	Friday	Saturday
			1	2	3	4
5	6	7	8	9	10 Michael Layman	11 Mary E. and Jeremiah ". McCloud
12 Gertrude ". Duncan	13	14	15	16	17 John Gipe Maria E. Miller Warner	18
19	20	21	22	23	24 John C. Warner	25
26 Sarah ".A. and Jacob W. Oberlander	27	28	29	30	31	

November 2014

	November 2014							December 2014					
S	M	T	W	T	F	S	S	M	T	W	T	F	S
						1		1	2	3	4	5	6
2	3	4	5	6	7	8	7	8	9	10	11	12	13
9	10	11	12	13	14	15	14	15	16	17	18	19	20
16	17	18	19	20	21	22	21	22	23	24	25	26	27
23	24	25	26	27	28	29	28	29	30	31			
30													

Sunday	Monday	Tuesday	Wednesday	Thursday	Friday	Saturday
2	3	4	5 Elmira E. Raymond Layman	6	7	
9	10 Anna M. Hamm Mille	11	12	13	14	1!
16	17	18	19	20 Rebecca J. Overlander Layman	21	2: Andrew Miller
23	24	25	26	27 Irvin W. Duncan	28	2!
30						

December 2014

December 2014

S	M	T	W	T	F	S
	1	2	3	4	5	6
7	8	9	10	11	12	13
14	15	16	17	18	19	20
21	22	23	24	25	26	27
28	29	30	31			

January 2015

S	M	T	W	T	F	S
				1	2	3
4	5	6	7	8	9	10
11	12	13	14	15	16	17
18	19	20	21	22	23	24
25	26	27	28	29	30	31

Sunday	Monday	Tuesday	Wednesday	Thursday	Friday	Saturday
		1	2 Hannah A.". Duncan Kerstetter	3	4 Rachel Neal Layman	5
6	7	8	9	10	11 Michael Layman	12
13	14	15	16	17	18 Jacob Gipe	19
20 Sarah ".A. Gipe Oberlander	21	22	23 Rachel Neal Layman	24	25	26
27 Jacob W. Oberlander	28 Peter Oberlander	29	30	31		

Chapter Six

The Sources, Afterword and Author's Bio.

Sources

Source Title: **12,000 Ancestors**

Citation: 12,000 Ancestors, Andrew Miller, reseracher Wonders waht's ahppended to her 12,000 relatives, June R Grove, Caryl Clarke, http://w2.ydr.com/story/security/74736/.

Miller, Andrew
Occu: Camp Security (York)

Source Title: **Anderson household**

Citation: Anderson household, 1910 United States Census, Northumberland Co, PA, ED 0115, Sheet 17A, ancestry.com & Microfilm, PA State Library, Hbg, PA.

Anderson, Mary "Mamie" Lucetta
Census: 1910 in Sunbury, Northumberland Co, PA

Citation: Anderson household, 1920 United States Census, Snyder Co, PA, Roll T625 1653, p 3B, ED 163, Image 0148, www.ancestry.com and 1920 United States Census, Snyder Co, PA, PA State Library microfilm image.

Anderson, Mary "Mamie" Lucetta
Census: 1920 in Monroe, Snyder Co, PA

Citation: Anderson household, 1920 United States Census, Snyder Co, PA, Roll T625 1653, p 3B, ED 163, Image 0148, www.ancestry.com and 1920 United States Census, Snyder Co, PA, PA State Library microfilm image.

Anderson, Mary "Mamie" Lucetta
Educ: 1920; School

Source Title: **Andreas Miller**

Citation: Andreas Miller, Miller family, Onetree, ancestry.com.

Miller, Andrew
Birth: March 14, 1752 in York Co, PA

Source Title: **Andrew Miller**

Citation: Andrew Miller, 1841 Rev War Census Ensuf Pensioner of PA, Eastern Dt, p 116, Barbara, homelybin@aol.com.

Miller, Andrew
Census: 1841 in Old Codorus, York Co, PA

Citation: Andrew Miller, 1842, York County Archives, York Co, PA.

Miller, Andrew
Death: November 22, 1842 in Codorus, York Co, PA

Citation: Andrew Miller, PA Census,1772-1890 Record, PA 1840 Pensioners List, Ronald V Jackson, AIS, ancestry.com.

Miller, Andrew
Miltry: Abt. 1780; American Revolution, Private PA Reg (York)

Citation: Andrew Miller, Probate files, 1842, Rep 338 York County Archives, York, PA, Deborah Hershey, Elizabethtown, PA, Dec 2008.

Miller, Andrew
Death: November 22, 1842 in Codorus, York Co, PA

Citation: Andrew Miller, Probate files, 1842, Rep 38, York County Archives, York, PA, Deborah Hershey, Elizabethtown, PA, Dec 2008.

Miller, Andrew
Prob: December 14, 1842 in Codorus, York Co, PA
Will: May 11, 1829 in Codorus, York Co, PA

Source Title: **Anna Charlotte Or**

Source Title: **Anna Charlotte Or (con't)**

Citation: Anna Charlotte Or, One tree, from WFT collection, trees.ancestry.com/owt, www.ancestry.com.

Dietz, Anna Charlotte
Marr: 1754 in York, York Co, PA
Birth: 1733 in PA

Geib, John Nicholas
Marr: 1754 in York, York Co, PA

Source Title: **Anna Maria Hamm**

Citation: Anna Maria Hamm, January 1, 1764, Christ Reformed, Littlestown, York (Adams) Co, PA.

Hamm, Anna Maria
Baptism: January 01, 1764 in York Co, PA

Citation: Anna Maria Hamm, November 10, 1763, Christ Reformed, Littlestown, York (Adams) Co, PA.

Hamm, Anna Maria
Birth: November 10, 1763 in York Co, PA

Source Title: **Baugher family information**

Citation: Baugher family information, Kim Morris.

Bager, John George William
Birth: April 15, 1750 in Simmern, Rhineland-Palatinate, Germany
Will: May 17, 1798 in Berwick, York Co, PA

Citation: Baugher family information, Tax lists 1779, 1780, 1781, 1782, 1783, York Co, PA, Kim Morris.

Bager, John George William
Res: Bet. 1775–1788 in Berwick, York Co, PA

Source Title: **Baugher household**

Citation: Baugher household, 1790 United States Census, York Co, PA, Roll M637-9, p 288, Image 0237, ancestry.com & Microfilm, PA State Library, Hbg, PA.

Bager, John George William
Census: 1790 in York Co, PA

Source Title: **Catherine Duncan**

Citation: Catherine Duncan, Death certificate, Northumberland Co County Register of Wills, Sunbury, PA.

McCloud, Catherine
Res: 1903 in 1014 R.R. Ave., Sunbury, Northumberland Co, PA
Birth: January 1847 in Hallowing Run, Northumberland Co, PA
Death: January 02, 1903 in Home, Sunbury, Northumberland Co, PA
Burial: January 06, 1903 in Old Sunbury Cemetery, Sunbury, Northumberland Co, PA

Source Title: **Charley Duncan**

Citation: Charley Duncan, Baptisms of Infants, Zion Evan Luth Register, 1851-1892, Sunbury, PA, p101.

Duncan, Charles "Charley"
Birth: June 26, 1882 in Sunbury, Northumberland Co, PA

Source Title: **Charlotte Layman**

Citation: Charlotte Layman, Duncan family information, Stephanie Gormley.

Layman, Charlotte "Lottie" Virginia

Source Title: **Charlotte Layman (con't)**

Citation: Charlotte Layman, Duncan family information, Stephanie Gormley.

Layman, Charlotte "Lottie" Virginia
Birth: May 12, 1881

Source Title: **David McCloud**

Citation: David McCloud, Probate files, 1864, Northumberland County Courthouse, Reg of Wills, Sunbury, Bk 5, p261, PA, Robyn Jackson, genealogylover@msn.com, 2008.

McCloud, David
Death: Bef. May 19, 1864 in Northumberland Co, PA
Prob: May 19, 1864 in Lower Augusta, Northumberland Co, PA

Source Title: **David R. Layman**

Citation: David R. Layman, Biography, source unknown.

Klein, Sarah
Death: Bet. 1850–1860 in Peach Bottom, York Co, PA
Kline, Henry
Occu: Abt. 1800; Cabinet maker

Source Title: **Donkert household**

Citation: Donkert household, 1880 United States Census, Northumberland Co, PA, ancestry.com & Microfilm, PA State Library, Hbg, PA.

Duncan, Frederick (Fritz Dankert)
Census: 1880 in Sunbury, Northumberland Co, PA
Duncan, William
Census: 1880 in Sunbury, Northumberland Co, PA

Citation: Donkert household, 1880 United States Census, Northumberland Co, PA, ancestry.com & Microfilm, PA State Library, Hbg, PA.

Duncan, Frederick (Fritz Dankert)
Res: 1880 in Short St., Sunbury, Northumberland Co, PA

Citation: Donkert household, 1880 United States Census, Northumberland Co, PA, FHL 1255164, Film T9-1164, p 521B, www.familysearch.org.

McCloud, Catherine
Occu: 1880; Keeping house

Source Title: **Duncan family information**

Citation: Duncan family information, 1870 United States Census, York Co, PA, Roll M593-1468, p 545, Image 700, ancestry.com & Microfilm, PA State Library, Hbg, PA.

Gipe, Sarah "Sallie" Ann
Marr: October 26, 1854 in St. Lukes (Stahleys) Lutheran, New Bridgeville, York Co, PA
Birth: 1834 in Chanceford, York Co, PA
Death: December 20, 1874 in Chanceford, York Co, PA
Burial: December 1874 in St. Lukes (Stahleys) Lutheran, New Bridgeville, York Co, PA
Oberlander, Jacob Warner
Marr: October 26, 1854 in St. Lukes (Stahleys) Lutheran, New Bridgeville, York Co, PA
Birth: 1819 in Chanceford, York Co, PA
Death: December 27, 1898 in Chanceford, York Co, PA
Oberlander, Michael Baugher
Marr: August 17, 1819 in First Trinity Reformed, Chanceford, York Co, PA
Birth: February 23, 1798 in Jefferson, Codorus, York Co, PA

Source Title: **Duncan family information (con't)**

Citation: Duncan family information, 1870 United States Census, York Co, PA, Roll M593-1468, p 545, Image 700, ancestry.com & Microfilm, PA State Library, Hbg, PA.

Oberlander, Michael Baugher
> Baptism: May 09, 1798 in St. Matthews Lutheran, Hanover, York Co, PA
> Relgn: Presbyterian

Warner, Maria Catherine
> Marr: August 17, 1819 in First Trinity Reformed, Chanceford, York Co, PA
> Death: 1848 in Chanceford, York Co, PA

Citation: Duncan family information, Jack Lehman, North Charleston, SC.

Anderson, Mary "Mamie" Lucetta
> Death: April 03, 1989 in Derry, Montour Co, PA
> Burial: April 05, 1989 in Pomfret Manor Cemetery, Sunbury, Northumberland Co, PA
> Occu: Abt. 1930; Domestic cook
> Relgn: Lutheran
> SSN: 1989; 170-26-9870

Duncan, Irvin Wilfred
> Birth: November 27, 1901 in Sunbury, Northumberland Co, PA
> Death: April 08, 1978 in Geisinger Medical Center, Mahoning, Montour Co, P
> Burial: April 11, 1978 in Pomfret Manor Cemetery, Sunbury, Northumberland Co, PA
> Occu: Abt. 1940; Produce Store Owner (Sunbury, Hummels Wharf)
> Relgn: Lutheran

Gipe, Sarah "Sallie" Ann
> Marr: October 26, 1854 in St. Lukes (Stahleys) Lutheran, New Bridgeville, York Co, PA
> Occu: 1870; Keeping house

Klein, Sarah
> Marr: June 28, 1818 in Trinity Lutheran, New Holland, Lancaster Co, PA
> Birth: 1796 in Manor, Lancaster Co, PA
> Death: Bet. 1850–1860 in Peach Bottom, York Co, PA
> Relgn: Lutheran

Layman, Joseph Pierce
> Birth: January 08, 1859 in Airville, York Co, PA
> Relgn: Methodist

Layman, Michael
> Marr: April 03, 1845 in Christ Lutheran, Elizabethtown, Lancaster Co, PA
> Birth: October 10, 1818 in Marietta, Lancaster Co, PA
> Death: May 17, 1892 in Lower Chanceford, York Co, PA
> Burial: May 1892 in Bethel United Methodist, Lower Chanceford, York Co, PA
> Relgn: Methodist

Layman, Michael
> Marr: June 28, 1818 in Trinity Lutheran, New Holland, Lancaster Co, PA
> Occu: Abt. 1830; Canal boatman
> Birth: Abt. 1795 in Milesburg, Northumberland (Centre) Co, PA
> Death: Abt. 1850 in Peach Bottom, York Co, PA
> Relgn: Methodist

Layman, Michael
> Occu: 1796; Carpenter
> Death: January 05, 1843 in Howard, Centre Co, PA
> Burial: 1843 in Howard Methodist Cemetery, Howard, Centre Co, PA

Source Title: **Duncan family information (con't)**

Citation: Duncan family information, Jack Lehman, North Charleston, SC.

Layman, Michael
- Miltry: Abt. 1780; American Revolution, Private 2nd PA Reg, ? Co, ? class (Philadelphia)
- Relgn: Methodist Episcopal

Miller, Maria Elizabeth
- Birth: October 17, 1777 in Cordorus, York Co, PA

Neal, Rachel
- Death: December 23, 1855 in Howard, Centre Co, PA
- Burial: 1855 in Howard Methodist Cemetery, Howard, Centre Co, PA
- Relgn: Methodist

Oberlander, Jacob Warner
- Marr: October 26, 1854 in St. Lukes (Stahleys) Lutheran, New Bridgeville, York Co, PA
- Census: 1860 in Chanceford, York Co, PA
- Census: 1880 in Chanceford, York Co, PA
- Birth: 1819 in Chanceford, York Co, PA
- Death: December 27, 1898 in Chanceford, York Co, PA
- Relgn: Lutheran

Overlander, Rebecca Jane
- Birth: October 1859 in Chanceford, York Co, PA
- Burial: November 23, 1921 in Pomfret Manor Cemetery, Sunbury, Northumberland Co, PA
- Relgn: Methodist

Raymond, Elmira Elizabeth
- Marr: April 03, 1845 in Christ Lutheran, Elizabethtown, Lancaster Co, PA
- Birth: January 17, 1824 in Maytown, York Co, PA
- Death: November 05, 1888 in Lower Chanceford, York Co, PA
- Burial: November 1888 in Bethel United Methodist, Lower Chanceford, York Co, PA
- Relgn: Methodist

Warner, John Christian
- Birth: October 24, 1775 in York Co, PA

Citation: Duncan family information, Stephanie Gormley, PA, 1989.

McCloud, Catherine
- Birth: March 05, 1849 in PA

Citation: Duncan family information, Stephanie Gormley.

Duncan, William
- Marr: April 13, 1899 in Sunbury, Northumberland Co, PA
- Birth: January 16, 1876 in Sunbury, Northumberland Co, PA

Layman, Charlotte "Lottie" Virginia
- Marr: April 13, 1899 in Sunbury, Northumberland Co, PA

Layman, Joseph Pierce
- Birth: January 08, 1859 in Airville, York Co, PA

Overlander, Rebecca Jane
- Birth: October 1859 in Chanceford, York Co, PA
- Death: November 20, 1921 in Hazleton State Hospital, Hazleton, Luzerne Co, PA

Source Title: **Duncan household**

Citation: Duncan household, 1900 United States Census, microfilm image, PA State Library.

Source Title: **Duncan household (con't)**

Citation: Duncan household, 1900 United States Census, microfilm image, PA State Library.

Duncan, William
    Census: 1900 in Sunbury, Northumberland Co, PA
        Occu: 1900; Blacksmith
            Res: 1900 in 929 Railroad Ave., Sunbury, Northumberland Co, PA
McCloud, Catherine
    Census: 1900 in Sunbury, Northumberland Co, PA
        Occu: 1900; Day laborer
            Res: 1900 in 927 Railroad Ave., Sunbury, Northumberland Co, PA

Citation: Duncan household, 1900 United States Census, microfilm image, PA State Library. Died Sunbury, PA, Duncan family information, Stephanie Gormley.

Layman, Charlotte "Lottie" Virginia
        Birth: May 1880

Citation: Duncan household, 1910 United States Census, Northumberland Co, PA, ED 0118, Visit 0155, ancestry.com & Microfilm, PA State Library, Hbg, PA.

Duncan, Irvin Wilfred
        Census: 1910 in Sunbury, Northumberland Co, PA
Layman, Charlotte "Lottie" Virginia
        Census: 1910 in Sunbury, Northumberland Co, PA

Citation: Duncan household, 1910 United States Census, Northumberland Co, PA, ED 0118, Visit 0155, ancestry.com & Microfilm, PA State Library, Hbg, PA.

Duncan, Irvin Wilfred
            Res: 1910 in 63 8th St., Sunbury, Northumbelrand, PA
        Educ: 1910; School
Layman, Charlotte "Lottie" Virginia
        Occu: 1900; Own income
            Res: 1910 in 63 8th St., Sunbury, Northumberland Co, PA

Source Title: **Duncan-Layman mariage record**

Citation: Duncan-Layman mariage record, #8855, Northumberland Co, PA, 1899, Northumberland Co County Register of Wills.

Duncan, William
        Birth: January 16, 1876 in Sunbury, Northumberland Co, PA

Source Title: **Duncan-Layman marriage record**

Citation: Duncan-Layman marriage record, #8855, Northumberland Co, PA, 1899, Northumberland Co County Register of Wills, Sunbury, PA.

Duncan, William
        Marr: April 13, 1899 in Sunbury, Northumberland Co, PA
Layman, Charlotte "Lottie" Virginia
        Marr: April 13, 1899 in Sunbury, Northumberland Co, PA

Citation: Duncan-Layman marriage record, #8855, Northumberland Co, PA, 1899, Northumberland Co County Register of Wills.

Duncan, William
        Occu: 1899; Blacksmith helper
            Res: 1899 in Sunbury, Northumberland Co, PA
Layman, Charlotte "Lottie" Virginia
        Birth: May 12, 1879 in Brogueville, York Co, PA
            Res: 1899 in Sunbury, Northumberland Co, PA

Citation: Duncan-Layman marriage record, April 20, 1899, Edward C. Eisley.

Duncan, William

Source Title: **Duncan-Layman marriage record (con't)**

Citation: Duncan-Layman marriage record, April 20, 1899, Edward C. Eisley.

Duncan, William
        Marr: April 13, 1899 in Sunbury, Northumberland Co, PA
Layman, Charlotte "Lottie" Virginia
        Marr: April 13, 1899 in Sunbury, Northumberland Co, PA

Source Title: **Dungan household**

Citation: Dungan household, 1870 United States Census, Northumberland Co, PA, ancestry.com & Microfilm, PA State Library, Hbg, PA.

Duncan, Frederick (Fritz Dankert)
        Occu: Bet. 1870–1880; Laborer

Source Title: **Dungard household**

Citation: Dungard household, 1870 United States Census, Northumberland Co, PA, ancestry.com & Microfilm, PA State Library, Hbg, PA.

Duncan, Frederick (Fritz Dankert)
        Census: 1870 in Sunbury, Northumberland Co, PA

Citation: Dungard household, 1870 United States Census, Northumberland Co, PA, ancestry.com & Microfilm, PA State Library, Hbg, PA.

Duncan, Frederick (Fritz Dankert)
        Propty: 1870 in $500

Source Title: **Elmira Layman**

Citation: Elmira Layman, Bethel ME Cemetery, p 151, Jerome K. Hively, Brogue, PA.

Raymond, Elmira Elizabeth
        Death: November 05, 1888 in Lower Chanceford, York Co, PA
        Burial: November 1888 in Bethel United Methodist, Lower Chanceford, York Co, PA

Source Title: **Geip family information**

Citation: Geip family information, December 9, 1992, Philip O'Leary, Willowick, OH 44095.

Geib, John Nicholas
        Birth: 1730 in Germany
        Relgn: Lutheran

Source Title: **Geipe household**

Citation: Geipe household, 1830 United States Census, York Co, PA ancestry.com & Microfilm, PA State Library, Hbg, PA.

Gipe, Jacob
        Census: 1830 in Upper Chanceford, York Co, PA (Geise)

Citation: Geipe household, 1830 United States Census, York Co, PA, ancestry.com & Microfilm, PA State Library, Hbg, PA.

Gipe, John
        Census: 1830 in Upper Chanceford, York Co, PA (Geise)

Source Title: **Geipp-Schreiberin marriage record**

Citation: Geipp-Schreiberin marriage record, Trinity Lutheran Church, Lancaster Co, PA German Society, volume VII, p 235.

Dietz, Anna Charlotte
        Relgn: Reformed

Source Title: **George H Layman**

Source Title: **George H Layman (con't)**

Citation: George H Layman, Commemorative Biographical Record of Cental PA, vol 1, Beers and Co, 1898, Jack Lehman, North Charleston, SC.

Layman, Michael
> Res: 1806 in Mountain Eagle, Centre Co, PA

Source Title: **George H Leyman**

Citation: George H Leyman, Commemorative Biographical Record, p 871-872.

Layman, Michael
> Miltry: Abt. 1780; American Revolution, Private 2nd PA Reg, ? Co, ? class (Philadelphia)
> Occu: Abt. 1790; Farmer

Source Title: **George William Baugher**

Citation: George William Baugher, Conrad Maul & and his Descendants, p 285, Adams Co County Historical Society.

Bager, John George William
> Birth: April 15, 1750 in Simmern, Rhineland-Palatinate, Germany

Source Title: **Gibe household**

Citation: Gibe household, 1850 United States Census, York Co, PA, Roll M432-839, p 40, Image 648, ancestry.com & Microfilm, PA State Library, Hbg, PA.

?, Elizabeth
> Census: 1850 in South ward York, York Co, PA

Source Title: **Gipe family information**

Citation: Gipe family information, Harry A. Diehl, Wilmington, DE.

Geib, John Nicholas
> Res: Abt. 1750 in Hempfield, Lancaster Co, PA

Source Title: **Gipe Family of Chanceford Twp., York Co**

Citation: Gipe Family of Chanceford Twp., York Co, 1997, Harry A. Diehl, p 1-5.

?, Elizabeth
> Birth: 1795 in PA

?, Elizabeth
> Birth: Abt. 1762
> Death: Bet. 1810–1820 in York Co, PA

Gipe, Jacob
> Birth: Abt. 1761 in York Co, PA
> Death: December 18, 1843 in Chanceford, York Co, PA
> Occu: Abt. 1800; Farmer
> Relgn: St. Lukes (Stahleys) Lutheran, New Bridgeville, York Co, PA

Gipe, John
> Birth: October 17, 1790 in York Co, PA
> Death: 1845 in Chanceford, York Co, PA

Source Title: **Gipe household**

Citation: Gipe household, 1810 United States Census, York Co, PA, ancestry.com & Microfilm, PA State Library, Hbg, PA.

Gipe, Jacob
> Census: 1810 in Chanceford, York Co, PA

Gipe, John
> Census: 1810 in father; Chanceford, York Co, PA w

Source Title: **Gipe household (con't)**

Citation: Gipe household, 1820 United States Census, York Co, PA, ancestry.com & Microfilm, PA State Library, Hbg, PA.

Gipe, Jacob
      Census: 1820 in Upper Chanceford, York Co, PA
Gipe, John
      Census: 1820 in Upper Chanceford, York Co, PA

Citation: Gipe household, 1840 United States Census, York Co, PA, ancestry.com & Microfilm, PA State Library, Hbg, PA.

Gipe, Jacob
      Census: 1840 in Chanceford, York Co, PA

Citation: Gipe household, 1840 United States Census, York Co, PA, Joanne Murry, rootsweb.com.

?, Elizabeth
      Census: 1840 in husband; Chanceford, York Co, PA w
Gipe, John
      Census: 1840 in Chanceford, York Co, PA

Source Title: **Gipe/Geib/Geiep,York Co, PA**

Citation: Gipe/Geib/Geiep,York Co, PA, Phil O'Leary.

Geib, John Nicholas
      Death: 1782 in Hellam, York Co, PA

Source Title: **Hannah Artilla Duncan**

Citation: Hannah Artilla Duncan, Baptisms of Infants, Zion Evan Luth Register, 1851-1892, Sunbury, PA, p94.

Duncan, Hannah Artila "Lilly"
      Birth: December 02, 1880 in Sunbury, Northumberland Co, PA

Source Title: **Hawkins household**

Citation: Hawkins household, 1900 United States Census, Northumberland Co, PA, ancestry.com & Microfilm, PA State Library, Hbg, PA.

Layman, Joseph Pierce
      Census: 1900 in Sunbury, Northumberland Co, PA (Laynon)

Citation: Hawkins household, 1920 United States Census, Cook, IL, ancestry.com & Microfilm, PA State Library, Hbg, PA.

Layman, Joseph Pierce
      Census: 1920 in Chicago, Cook, IL
        Occu: 1920; Store room (Packing House)
         Res: 1920 in Blackstone Avenue, Chicago, Cook, IL
Overlander, Rebecca Jane
      Census: 1920 in Chicago, Cook, IL

Source Title: **Henry Klein**

Citation: Henry Klein, History of Lancaster County, F Ellis & S Evans, p 960, Lancaster County Historical Society.

Kline, Henry
        Res: 1815 in Safe Harbor, Conestoga, Lancaster Co, PA

Citation: Henry Klein, June 18, 1832, December 1832, Abstracts of Lancaster County Wills, Lancaster Co, PA.

Kline, Henry
        Prob: June 18, 1832 in Lancaster Co, PA

Citation: Henry Klein, WFT, Volume 43, Tree 971.

Source Title: **Henry Klein (con't)**

Citation: Henry Klein, WFT, Volume 43, Tree 971.

Kline, Henry
> Death: March 1832 in Safe Harbor, Conestoga, Lancaster Co, PA

Surr, Catherine
> Death: Bet. 1810–1820 in Safe Harbor, Conestoga, Lancaster Co, PA

Source Title: **Henry Neal**

Citation: Henry Neal, Notebooks at the Historical Room, Bellefonte Spangle Collection, 1802, Jack Lehman, North Charleston, SC.

Neal, Henry
> Res: Bet. 1802–1809 in Potter Tp, Centre Co, PA

Citation: Henry Neal, Notebooks at the Historical Room, Bellefonte Spangle Collection, 1806, Jack Lehman, North Charleston, SC.

Neal, Henry
> Res: Bet. 1802–1809 in Potter Tp, Centre Co, PA

Citation: Henry Neal, Notebooks at the Historical Room, Bellefonte Spangle Collection, 1809, Jack Lehman, North Charleston, SC.

Neal, Henry
> Res: Bet. 1802–1809 in Potter Tp, Centre Co, PA

Citation: Henry Neal, Notebooks at the Historical Room, Bellefonte Spangle Collection, 1810, Jack Lehman, North Charleston, SC.

Neal, Henry
> Occu: 1810; Trade

Citation: Henry Neal, Notebooks at The Historical Room, Bellefonte Spangle Collection, Jack Lehman, North Charleston, SC.

Neal, Henry
> Occu: Bet. 1802–1806; Tailor

Source Title: **Henry Neel**

Citation: Henry Neel, Tax list, 1796, Annals of Buffalo Valley, p 301?.

Neal, Henry
> Occu: 1796; Tailor

Source Title: **Irvin Duncan**

Citation: Irvin Duncan, April 1978, PA, Social Security Death Index, www.familysearch.org.

Duncan, Irvin Wilfred
> Res: 1978 in Blue Hill, Dogtown, Jackson, Kantz, Kratzerville, Penn Avon, Salem, Selinsgrove, Verdilla, all Snyder, PA
> Death: April 08, 1978 in Geisinger Medical Center, Mahoning, Montour Co, P
> SSN: 1978; 209-24-9584

Citation: Irvin Duncan, Pomfret Manor Cemetery, Sam Derr, Sunbury, PA, lot 130-B.

Duncan, Irvin Wilfred
> Burial: April 11, 1978 in Pomfret Manor Cemetery, Sunbury, Northumberland Co, PA

Source Title: **Irvin Francis Duncan**

Citation: Irvin Francis Duncan, Birth record, Northumberland Co County Courthouse, Register of Wills, Sunbury, PA.

Duncan, Irvin Wilfred
> Birth: November 27, 1901 in Sunbury, Northumberland Co, PA
> Res: 1901 in Susquehanna Ave., Sunbury, Northumberland Co, PA

Source Title: **Irvin Francis Duncan death certificate**

Citation: Irvin Francis Duncan death certificate, #0030831, Northumberland Co, PA, Department of Vital Records, New Castle, PA.

Duncan, Irvin Wilfred

  Occu: 1978; Fruit & Produce

   Res: 1978 in RD 2, Selinsgrove, Snyder, PA 17870

   Death: April 08, 1978 in Geisinger Medical Center, Mahoning, Montour Co, P

   Burial: April 11, 1978 in Pomfret Manor Cemetery, Sunbury, Northumberland Co, PA

  CasDth: Squamous cell carcinoma of lung w/pulmonary edema w/ASCVD.

   SSN: 1978; 209-24-9584

  Funeral: April 11, 1978 in M. Quay Olley [Olley-Gotlob] Funeral Home, 539 Race St., Sunbury, Northumberland Co, PA

Citation: Irvin Francis Duncan death certificate, Funeral death record, Olley-Gotlob Funeral Home, Sunbury, PA.

Duncan, Irvin Wilfred

  Member: Hummels Wharf Fire Co, Finanacial & recording Sec., Rescue Hose Co Sby.

Source Title: **Irvin W Duncan**

Citation: Irvin W Duncan, Social Seurity numident record, application for SS-5, SSA, Nov 2006, Baltimore, MD.

Duncan, Irvin Wilfred

   Res: 1963 in Sunbury, Northumberland Co, PA

Source Title: **Irvin Wilfred Francis Duncan**

Citation: Irvin Wilfred Francis Duncan, Funeral death record, Olley-Gotlob Funeral Home, Sunbury, PA.

Duncan, Irvin Wilfred

  Relgn: United Methodist

Source Title: **Jacob Gipe**

Citation: Jacob Gipe, 1844, Probate Invent. Index York County, PA, 1749-1850, Chanceford, York County, PA, Gert Mysliwski,gert@foothill.net.

Gipe, Jacob

  Death: December 18, 1843 in Chanceford, York Co, PA

Citation: Jacob Gipe, April 4, 1844, bk 20, p 444, Will Records, York County, PA.

Gipe, Jacob

  Prob: Bet. April 04, 1844–December 18, 1845 in Chanceford, York Co, PA

Citation: Jacob Gipe, Probate files, 1845, Rep 36, York County Archives, York, PA, Deborah Hershey, Elizabethtown, PA, Dec 2008.

Gipe, Jacob

  Prob: Bet. April 04, 1844–December 18, 1845 in Chanceford, York Co, PA

Source Title: **Jacob Gype**

Citation: Jacob Gype, Tax list, 1783, Windsor, York County, PA.

Gipe, Jacob

   Res: 1783 in Windsor, York Co, PA

Source Title: **Jacob Loyman**

Citation: Jacob Loyman, Probate files, Bk E, vol 1, p196, Lancaster County Archives Division, Lancaster Co Courthouse, Lancaster, PA, Deborah Hershey, Elizabethtown, PA, Mar 2008.

Loyman, John Jacob

Source Title: **Jacob Loyman (con't)**

Citation: Jacob Loyman, Probate files, Bk E, vol 1, p196, Lancaster County Archives Division, Lancaster Co Courthouse, Lancaster, PA, Deborah Hershey, Elizabethtown, PA, Mar 2008.

Loyman, John Jacob
       Will: February 06, 1785 in Conestoga Tp, Lancaster Co, PA

Source Title: **Jacob Oberlander**

Citation: Jacob Oberlander, 1816, Probate Invent. Index York County, PA, 1749-1850, Chanceford, York County, PA, Gert Mysliwski,gert@foothill.net.

Oberlander, Jacob
       Prob: Bet. May 14–December 18, 1816 in Chanceford, York Co, PA .

Citation: Jacob Oberlander, Probate files, 1816, Rep 39, York County Archives, York, PA, Deborah Hershey, Elizabethtown, PA, Dec 2008.

Oberlander, Jacob
       Prob: Bet. May 14–December 18, 1816 in Chanceford, York Co, PA

Citation: Jacob Oberlander, Saul/Kagy/Weisenauer/gqinner Family, Mary Ross, ross.8@osu.edu, awt.ancestry.com/.

Baugher, Susan
       Birth: 1773 in Berwick, York Co, PA
       Death: April 21, 1814 in Chanceford, York Co, PA

Oberlander, Jacob
       Death: April 12, 1816 in Chanceford, York Co, PA

Oberlander, Peter
       Death: December 28, 1780 in Heidelberg, Lancaster (Lebanon) Co, PA

Source Title: **Joahnn Jacob Leiman**

Citation: Joahnn Jacob Leiman, PA Census, 1772-1890, Philadelphia, PA, www.ancestry.com.

Loyman, John Jacob
       Res: Bet. 1764–1765 in Philadelphia, PA

Source Title: **Johan Nicholas Geipp**

Citation: Johan Nicholas Geipp, Geipp family, Onetree, ancestry.com.

Dietz, Anna Charlotte
       Death: Abt. 1782 in York Co, PA

Source Title: **Johann Christian Warner**

Citation: Johann Christian Warner, March 10, 1840, June 22, 1842, bk s, p 255.

Warner, John Christian
       Will: June 22, 1842

Source Title: **Johann Christian Werner**

Citation: Johann Christian Werner, #262-385, Calender of Vitals records of the Counties of York & Adams Co.

Warner, John Christian
       Birth: October 24, 1775 in York Co, PA
         Baptism: November 19, 1775 in St. Jacobs (Stone) Union, Glenville, York Co, PA

Citation: Johann Christian Werner, 1775, St. Jacobs Lutheran & Reformed Church, Codorus, York Co, PA, Early York County Births, J. Humphrey.

Warner, John Christian
         Baptism: November 19, 1775 in St. Jacobs (Stone) Union, Glenville, York Co, PA

Source Title: **Johann Christian Werner (con't)**

Citation: Johann Christian Werner, St. Jacobs (Stone) UCC Church, Doris Miller, Glenville, PA.

Warner, John Christian
        Birth: October 24, 1775 in York Co, PA
           Baptism: November 19, 1775 in St. Jacobs (Stone) Union, Glenville, York Co, PA

Source Title: **Johann Jacob Leiman**

Citation: Johann Jacob Leiman, Passenger and Immigration Lists Index, 1500-1900, myfamily.com, P. William Filby, ancestry.com.

Loyman, John Jacob
        Immigr: Abt. 1764; Germany to USA

Source Title: **John Bager**

Citation: John Bager, York County, PA Wills, 1749-1819, www.ancestry.com.

Bager, John George William
        Res: Bet. 1775–1788 in Berwick, York Co, PA

Source Title: **John George Bager (father)**

Citation: John George Bager (father), Passenger and Immigration Lists Index, 1500-1900, myfamily.com, P. William Filby, ancestry.com.

Bager, John George William
        Immigr: October 23, 1752; Germany to USA (ship Bawley, w/father)

Source Title: **John Reiman**

Citation: John Reiman, York Co, PA Will index, c/o Gert Mysliwski, gert@foothill.net.

Reiman, John
        Will: 1841 in York, York Co, PA

Source Title: **John Werner**

Citation: John Werner, July 20, 1805, August 16, 1805, Abstracts of York County Wills 1749-1819, Family Line Publication, 1995, L. Gohn lbeth@erols.com.

Werner, John George
        Will: July 10, 1805 in Codorus, York Co, PA

Citation: John Werner, Probate files, 1805, Rep 47, York County Archives, York, PA, Deborah Hershey, Elizabethtown, PA, Dec 2008.

Werner, John George
        Prob: August 16, 1805 in Codorus, York Co, PA
        Will: July 10, 1805 in Codorus, York Co, PA

Source Title: **Joseph P Leyman**

Citation: Joseph P Leyman, Evergreen Cemtery, Index files and lot lists, #5435, Lot SG 157, Maple Gr Pt 6, vault 5/9/box, permit #4976, Chiacgo, IL.

Layman, Joseph Pierce
        Burial: February 22, 1924 in Evergreen Cemetery, Chicago, IL

Source Title: **Joseph Pierce Layman**

Citation: Joseph Pierce Layman, death record, Illinois Statewide Death Index, 1916-1950, www.cyberdriveillinois.com/GenealogyMWeb/ODPHdeathsearch.

Layman, Joseph Pierce
        Res: 1924 in Chicago, Cook Co, IL
        Death: February 20, 1924 in Chicago, Cook Co, IL

Citation: Joseph Pierce Layman, State of IL, Dept of Public Health, DVS, Reg #4976, Primary Dt #3104, Cook, IL, Feb 1924.

Source Title: **Joseph Pierce Layman (con't)**

Citation: Joseph Pierce Layman, State of IL, Dept of Public Health, DVS, Reg #4976, Primary Dt #3104, Cook, IL, Feb 1924.

Layman, Joseph Pierce
  Occu: 1924; Stationary & Locomotive Engineer
  Res: 1924 in 908 W 70th St, Chicago, Cook Co, IL
  Death: February 20, 1924 in Chicago, Cook Co, IL
  Burial: February 22, 1924 in Evergreen Cemetery, Chicago, IL
  CasDth: Valvular heart disease (aorotic) w/chronic nephritis & cystitis
  Funeral: February 22, 1924 in JJ Sullivan

Source Title: **June Delores Gerrick Pedigree Chart**

Citation: June Delores Gerrick Pedigree Chart, June G Herr, 7501 15th Avenue N, St. Petersburg, FL 33710.

Dietz, Anna Charlotte
  Birth: 1733 in PA

Source Title: **Klein hosusehold**

Citation: Klein hosusehold, 1820 United States Census, Lancaster Co, PA, ancestry.com & Microfilm, PA State Library, Hbg, PA.

Klein, Sarah
  Census: 1820 in Manor, Lancaster Co, PA

Source Title: **Kline household**

Citation: Kline household, 1810 United States Census, Lancaster Co, PA, ancestry.com & Microfilm, PA State Library, Hbg, PA.

Kline, Henry
  Census: 1810 in Hempfield, Lancaster Co, PA

Citation: Kline household, 1820 United States Census, Lancaster Co, PA, ancestry.com & Microfilm, PA State Library, Hbg, PA.

Kline, Henry
  Census: 1820 in West Hempfield, Lancaster Co, PA

Citation: Kline household, 1830 United States Census, Lancaster Co, PA, ancestry.com.

Kline, Henry
  Census: 1830

Source Title: **Lausman household**

Citation: Lausman household, 18000 United States Census, Northumberland Co, PA, Roll M32-37, p 852, Image 200, ancestry.com.

Layman, Michael
  Census: 1800

Source Title: **Layman household**

Citation: Layman household, 1800 United States Census, Centre Co, PA, ancestry.com & Microfilm, PA State Library, Hbg, PA.

Layman, Michael
  Census: 1800 in parents; w

Citation: Layman household, 1810 United States Census, Centre Co, PA, ancestry.com & Microfilm, PA State Library, Hbg, PA.

Layman, Michael
  Census: 1810 in Howard, Centre Co, PA

Citation: Layman household, 1850 United States Census, Centre Co, PA, ancestry.com & Microfilm, PA State Library, Hbg, PA.

Neal, Rachel

Source Title: **Layman household (con't)**

Citation: Layman household, 1850 United States Census, Centre Co, PA, ancestry.com & Microfilm, PA State Library, Hbg, PA.

Neal, Rachel
    Census: 1850 in Howard, Centre Co, PA (son John Layman)

Citation: Layman household, 1850 United States Census, Centre Co, PA, ancestry.com & Microfilm, PA State Library, Hbg, PA.

Neal, Rachel
    Propty: 1850 in $450
    Occu: 1850; House & lot?

Source Title: **Layman/Lehman family information**

Citation: Layman/Lehman family information, Files, NCHS, The Hunter House, Sunbury, PA.

Layman, Joseph Pierce
    Death: February 20, 1924 in Chicago, Cook Co, IL

Source Title: **Laymen household**

Citation: Laymen household, 1910 United States Census, Northumberland Co, PA, ED 0114, Visit 0085, ancestry.com & Microfilm, PA State Library, Hbg, PA.

Overlander, Rebecca Jane
    Census: 1910 in Sunbury, Northumberland Co, PA (Laymer)

Citation: Laymen household, 1910 United States Census, Northumberland Co, PA, ED 0114, Visit 0085, ancestry.com & Microfilm, PA State Library, Hbg, PA.

Overlander, Rebecca Jane
    Res: 1910 in 517 Chestnut St., Sunbury, Northumberland Co, PA

Source Title: **Laynon household**

Citation: Laynon household, 1900 United States Census, Northumberland Co, PA, ancestry.com & Microfilm, PA State Library, Hbg, PA.

Layman, Joseph Pierce
    Occu: 1900; Brakeman (RR)
    Res: 1900 in 209 3rd St., Sunbury, Northumberland Co, PA

Source Title: **Lehman-Klein marriage record**

Citation: Lehman-Klein marriage record, June 28, 1818, Church Book records 4.

Klein, Sarah
    Marr: June 28, 1818 in Trinity Lutheran, New Holland, Lancaster Co, PA
Layman, Michael
    Marr: June 28, 1818 in Trinity Lutheran, New Holland, Lancaster Co, PA

Citation: Lehman-Klein marriage record, Marriages at Trinity Lutheran Church, Lancaster Co, PA, Joan E. Kahler, Charles.Kahler@worldnet.att.net.

Klein, Sarah
    Marr: June 28, 1818 in Trinity Lutheran, New Holland, Lancaster Co, PA
Layman, Michael
    Marr: June 28, 1818 in Trinity Lutheran, New Holland, Lancaster Co, PA

Source Title: **Lehman-Oberlander marriage**

Citation: Lehman-Oberlander marriage, source unknown.

Layman, Joseph Pierce
    Marr: 1877 in Chanceford, York Co, PA
Overlander, Rebecca Jane
    Marr: 1877 in Chanceford, York Co, PA

Source Title: **Leyman family information**

Source Title: **Leyman family information (con't)**

Citation: Leyman family information, source unknown.

> ?, Anna Margaret
>> Death: 1786 in Lancaster Co, PA
>
> Layman, Michael
>> Res: 1847 in Relocated to York County
>
> Layman, Michael
>> Res: Bet. 1795–1803 in Northumberland (Union) Co, PA
>> Miltry: Abt. 1780; American Revolution, Private 2nd PA Reg, ? Co, ? class (Philadelphia)
>> Occu: Abt. 1790; Farmer
>
> Neal, Rachel
>> Birth: December 04, 1765 in Buffalo Valley, Lancaster (Union) Co, PA

Citation: Leyman family information, Tax list, 1796, West Buffalo, Northumberland (Union) Co, PA.

> Layman, Michael
>> Occu: 1796; Carpenter

Citation: Leyman family information, Tax list, 1796, West Buffalo, Northumberland (Union) Co, PA.

> Layman, Michael
>> Res: 1796 in West Buffalo, Northumberland (Union) Co, PA

Citation: Leyman family information, Tax list, 1799, Mifflinburg, Union Co, PA.

> Layman, Michael
>> Res: 1799 in Mifflinburg, Northumberland (Union) Co, PA
>
> Neal, Henry
>> Res: 1799 in Mifflinburg, Northumberland (Union) Co, PA

Source Title: **Leyman household**

Citation: Leyman household, 1840 United States Census, Centre Co, PA, ancestry.com & Microfilm, PA State Library, Hbg, PA.

> Layman, Michael
>> Census: 1840 in Howard, Centre Co, PA (Leyman)

Source Title: **Limmen household**

Citation: Limmen household, 1790 United States Census, Northumberland Co, PA ancestry.com & Microfilm, PA State Library, Hbg, PA.

> Layman, Michael
>> Census: 1790 in parents; w

Source Title: **Lottie Duncan**

Citation: Lottie Duncan, Pomfret Manor Cemetery, Sam Derr, Sunbury, PA, lot 130-B.

> Layman, Charlotte "Lottie" Virginia
>> Burial: March 03, 1936 in Pomfret Manor Cemetery, Sunbury, Northumberland Co, PA

Source Title: **Lottie V Willard death certificate**

Citation: Lottie V Willard death certificate, File #29987, Reg #19, #3505042, February 1936, Department of Vital Records, New Castle, PA.

> Layman, Charlotte "Lottie" Virginia
>> Funeral: 1936 in F.K. Sutton, Selinsgrove, Snyder Co, PA

Source Title: **Lottie V. Willard**

Source Title: **Lottie V. Willard (con't)**

Citation: Lottie V. Willard, death certificate, File #29987, Reg #19, #3505042, February 1936, Department of Vital Records, New Castle, PA.

Layman, Charlotte "Lottie" Virginia
   Birth: May 12, 1879 in Brogueville, York Co, PA
   Death: February 29, 1936 in at Irvin's home, Monroe, Snyder Co, PA
   Burial: March 03, 1936 in Pomfret Manor Cemetery, Sunbury, Northumberland Co, PA
      Occu: 1936; Retired

Layman, Joseph Pierce
   Birth: January 08, 1859 in Airville, York Co, PA

Citation: Lottie V. Willard, Lottie Duncan, Pomfret Manor Cemetery, Sam Derr, Sunbury, PA, lot 130-B.

Layman, Charlotte "Lottie" Virginia
   CasDth: Cerebral hemorrhage w/interstitial nephritis

Source Title: **Lyman household**

Citation: Lyman household, 1810 United States Census, Centre Co, PA, ancestry.com & Microfilm, PA State Library, Hbg, PA.

Layman, Michael
   Census: 1810 in Howard, Centre Co, PA (Lyman)

Citation: Lyman household, 1820 United States Census, Centre Co, PA, ancestry.com & Microfilm, PA State Library, Hbg, PA.

Layman, Michael
   Census: 1820 in Howard, Centre Co, PA (Lyman)

Citation: Lyman household, 1820 United States Census, Centre Co, PA, ancestry.com & Microfilm, PA State Library, Hbg, PA.

Layman, Michael
   Occu: 1820; Manufacturing

Citation: Lyman household, 1850 United States Census, York Co, PA, Roll M432-839, p 206, Image 180, ancestry.com & Microfilm, PA State Library, Hbg, PA.

Layman, Michael
   Census: 1850 in Lower Chanceford, York Co, PA
      Occu: Bet. 1850–1860; Boatman

Layman, Michael
   Census: 1850 in Peach Bottom, York Co, PA (Lyman)
      Occu: 1850; Laborer

Citation: Lyman household, 1860 United States Census, York Co, PA, ancestry.com & Microfilm, PA State Library, Hbg, PA.

Layman, Joseph Pierce
   Census: 1860 in Lower Chanceford, York Co, PA

Layman, Michael
   Census: 1860 in Lower Chanceford, York Co, PA

Citation: Lyman household, 1860 United States Census, York Co, PA, ancestry.com & Microfilm, PA State Library, Hbg, PA.

Layman, Michael
   Propty: 1860 in $600 + $675

Citation: Lyman household, 1870 United States Census, York Co, PA, Roll M593 1468, p 545, Image 700, ancestry.com & Microfilm, PA State Library, Hbg, PA.

Layman, Joseph Pierce
   Census: 1870 in Lower Chanceford, York Co, PA

Raymond, Elmira Elizabeth
   Census: 1870 in Lower Chanceford, York Co, PA

Source Title: **Lyman household (con't)**

Citation: Lyman household, 1870 United States Census, York Co, PA, Roll M593-1468, p 545, Image 700, ancestry.com & Microfilm, PA State Library, Hbg, PA.

Layman, Joseph Pierce
      Educ: 1870; School

Layman, Michael
        Propty: 1870 in $3000 + $2500
          Occu: 1870; Farmer

Raymond, Elmira Elizabeth
          Occu: Bet. 1870–1880; Keeping house

Citation: Lyman household, 1870 United States Census, York Co, PA, Roll M593-1468, p 545, Image 700, ancestry.com & Microfilm, PA State Library, Hbg, PA.

Layman, Michael
          Census: 1870 in Lower Chanceford, York Co, PA
          Occu: Abt. 1835; Farmer

Citation: Lyman household, 1880 United States Census, York Co, PA, FHL 1255208, Film T9-1208, p 640D, www.familysearch.org.

Layman, Michael
          Census: 1880 in Lower Chanceford, York Co, PA
          Occu: 1880; Lanlord (Landlord)

Raymond, Elmira Elizabeth
          Occu: Bet. 1870–1880; Keeping house

Source Title: **Lymon household**

Citation: Lymon household, 1830 United States Census, Centre Co, PA, Roll M19 165, p 433, Image 849, ancestry.com & Microfilm, PA State Library, Hbg, PA.

Layman, Michael
          Census: 1830 in Howard, Centre Co, PA (Lymon)

Source Title: **Mamie Duncan**

Citation: Mamie Duncan, #0078833, #069201, April 1989, Department of Vital Record, New Castle, PA.

Anderson, Mary "Mamie" Lucetta
          SSN: 1989; 170-26-9870

Citation: Mamie Duncan, April 1989, PA, Social Security Death Index, www.familysearch.org.

Anderson, Mary "Mamie" Lucetta
          Birth: April 11, 1908 in At home, Sunbury, Northumberland Co, PA
          Death: April 03, 1989 in Derry, Montour Co, PA
          SSN: 1989; 170-26-9870

Citation: Mamie Duncan, Pomfret Manor Cemetery, Sam Derr, Sunbury, PA, lot 130-B.

Anderson, Mary "Mamie" Lucetta
          Burial: April 05, 1989 in Pomfret Manor Cemetery, Sunbury, Northumberland Co, PA

Source Title: **Mamie L Duncan**

Citation: Mamie L Duncan, Probate file, 47-89-85, microfiche, Montour County Courthouse, Office of the Reg and Recorder, Danville, PA, Norman Nicol, ndnicol@epix.net, Mar 2008.

Anderson, Mary "Mamie" Lucetta
          Death: April 03, 1989 in Derry, Montour Co, PA
          Prob: February 05, 1990 in Montour Co, PA

Citation: Mamie L Duncan, Social Seurity numident record, application for SS-5, SSA, Nov 2006, Baltimore, MD.

Anderson, Mary "Mamie" Lucetta

Source Title: **Mamie L Duncan (con't)**

Citation: Mamie L Duncan, Social Seurity numident record, application for SS-5, SSA, Nov 2006, Baltimore, MD.

Anderson, Mary "Mamie" Lucetta
Res: Bet. 1969–1970 in Sunbury, Northumberland Co, PA

Source Title: **Mamie Lucetta Duncan**

Citation: Mamie Lucetta Duncan, #0078833, #069201, April 1989, Department of Vital Record, New Castle, PA.

Anderson, Mary "Mamie" Lucetta
Res: 1989 in RD 2, Box 574, Danville, Mountour, PA 17821

Source Title: **Mamie Lucetta Duncan death certificate**

Citation: Mamie Lucetta Duncan death certificate, #0078833, #069201, April 1989, Department of Vital Record, New Castle, PA.

Anderson, Mary "Mamie" Lucetta
Birth: April 11, 1908 in At home, Sunbury, Northumberland Co, PA
Death: April 03, 1989 in Derry, Montour Co, PA
Burial: April 05, 1989 in Pomfret Manor Cemetery, Sunbury, Northumberland Co, PA
CasDth: Carcinoma of lung w/ metastasis
Funeral: 1989 in VL Seebold, 601 N High St, Selinsgrove, Snyder Co, PA

Source Title: **Mamie Luzetta Anderson**

Citation: Mamie Luzetta Anderson, #061660-1908, 04-13-1908, Northumberland Co, PA, Department of Vital Records, New Castle, PA.

Anderson, Mary "Mamie" Lucetta
Birth: April 11, 1908 in At home, Sunbury, Northumberland Co, PA

Source Title: **Margaret Layman**

Citation: Margaret Layman, Estate Inventory, 1786, b86, f8, Marge Bardeen, 2006, Lancaster County Historical Society, Lancaster, PA.

?, Anna Margaret
Prob: 1786 in Lancaster Co, PA

Source Title: **Maria Catharina Werner**

Citation: Maria Catharina Werner, baptismal record, St Jacobs Lutheran Church, Vicki Kessler, Secretary, saintjacobslutheranchurch@msn.com.

Warner, Maria Catherine
Birth: March 21, 1798 in Hanover, York Co, PA
Baptism: Bet. May 07–09 1798 in St. Jacobs (Stone) Union, Glenville, York Co, PA

Source Title: **Maria Catharine Warner Oberlander**

Citation: Maria Catharine Warner Oberlander, findagave.com.

Warner, Maria Catherine
Burial: 1848 in Saint Lukes Evangelical Lutheran Cemetery, New Bridgeville, PA

Source Title: **Maria Catherine Werner**

Citation: Maria Catherine Werner, St. Jacobs (Stone) UCC Church, Doris Miller, Glenville, PA.

Warner, Maria Catherine
Baptism: Bet. May 07–09 1798 in St. Jacobs (Stone) Union, Glenville, York Co, PA

Source Title: **Mary Lucetta Anderson**

Citation: Mary Lucetta Anderson, Memoranda, Bob Anderson, PA, rmorris@ptd.net.

Anderson, Mary "Mamie" Lucetta
   Birth: April 11, 1908 in At home, Sunbury, Northumberland Co, PA

Source Title: **McCloud household**

Citation: McCloud household, 1860 United States Census, Northumberland Co, PA, ancestry.com & Microfilm, PA State Library, Hbg, PA.

McCloud, Catherine
   Census: 1860 in Sunbury, Northumberland Co, PA (Mary)

Citation: McCloud household, 1860 United States Census, Northumberland Co, PA, Series M653, Roll 1149, p 71, ancestry.com & Microfilm, PA State Library, Hbg, PA.

McCloud, David
   Census: 1860 in Lower Augusta, Northumberland Co, PA
      Occu: Bet. 1850–1860; Laborer

Citation: McCloud household, 1860 United States Census, Northumberland Co, PA, Series M653, Roll 1149, p 71, ancestry.com & Microfilm, PA State Library, Hbg, PA.

McCloud, David
   Propty: 1860 in $100 + $40

Citation: McCloud household, 1870 United States Census, Northumberland Co, PA, ancestry.com & Microfilm, PA State Library, Hbg, PA.

?, Mary
   Census: 1870 in Lower Augusta, Northumberland Co, PA

Citation: McCloud household, 1870 United States Census, Northumberland Co, PA, ancestry.com & Microfilm, PA State Library, Hbg, PA.

?, Mary
   Propty: 1870 in $150 + $100

Citation: McCloud household, 1880 United States Census, Northumberland Co, PA, ancestry.com & Microfilm, PA State Library, Hbg, PA.

?, Mary
   Occu: 1880; Keeping house

Citation: McCloud household, 1880 United States Census, Northumberland Co, PA, ancestry.com & Microfilm, PA State Library, Hbg, PA.

?, Mary
   Census: 1880 in Lower Augusta, Northumberland Co, PA

Source Title: **McCloud-Frye**

Citation: McCloud-Frye, Marriage, Northumberland County, SS, #2856, Register & Recorder, Sunbury, PA, Oct 1890, Market St, Sunbury, PA.

Frye, Mary E
   Marr: October 11, 1890 in Sunbury, Northumberland Co, PA
McCloud, Jeremiah "Jerry"
   Marr: October 11, 1890 in Sunbury, Northumberland Co, PA

Source Title: **McLeod household**

Citation: McLeod household, 1850 United States Census, Northumberland Co, PA, ancestry.com & Microfilm, PA State Library, Hbg, PA.

McCloud, David
   Propty: 1850 in $100
      Occu: Bet. 1850–1860; Laborer

Citation: McLeod household, 1850 United States Census, Northumberland Co, PA, ancestry.com & Microfilm, PA State Library, Hbg, PA.

McCloud, David

Source Title: **McLeod household (con't)**

Citation: McLeod household, 1850 United States Census, Northumberland Co, PA, ancestry.com & Microfilm, PA State Library, Hbg, PA.

McCloud, David
    Census: 1850 in Lower Augusta, Northumberland Co, PA (Daniel Mcleod)

Source Title: **Melinda Duncan**

Citation: Melinda Duncan, Cemetery record, Apr 1933, A genealogists Guide to Burials in Northumberland Co, PA, Vol I, Meiser & Meiser, 1989.

Duncan, Melinda E
    Birth: January 17, 1871 in Sunbury, Northumberland Co, PA
    Death: April 27, 1933 in Sunbury, Northumberland Co, PA

Source Title: **Mich. Leman**

Citation: Mich. Leman, April 26, 1781, Commonwealth of PA, PA Historical & Museum Society.

Layman, Michael
    Res: 1781 in Philadelphia, PA

Citation: Mich. Leman, Commonwealth of PA, PA Historical & Museum Society.

Layman, Michael
    Miltry: Abt. 1780; American Revolution, Private 2nd PA Reg, ? Co, ? class (Philadelphia)

Source Title: **Michael Layman**

Citation: Michael Layman, Bethel ME Cemetery, p 151, Jerome K. Hively, Brogue, PA.

Layman, Michael
    Birth: October 10, 1818 in Marietta, Lancaster Co, PA
    Death: May 17, 1892 in Lower Chanceford, York Co, PA

Citation: Michael Layman, List of Taxables, p 318, Jack Lehman, North Charleston, SC.

Layman, Michael
    Occu: 1799; Joiner

Source Title: **Michael Leyman**

Citation: Michael Leyman, Baptism/Birth, Southeastern Pennsylvania, 1600-1800 Index, Fillows4@aol.com.

Layman, Michael
    Birth: December 11, 1764 in Philadelphia, Philadelphia, PA
    Baptism: January 12, 1765 in St. Michael's Zion Lutheran Church, Philadelphia, Philadelphia, PA

Citation: Michael Leyman, Commemorative Biographical Record, Northern PA.

Layman, Michael
    Birth: December 11, 1764 in Philadelphia, Philadelphia, PA
    Occu: Abt. 1790; Farmer
    Relgn: Methodist Episcopal

Citation: Michael Leyman, Howard Cemetery, Centre Co, PA, p 5.

Layman, Michael
    Death: January 05, 1843 in Howard, Centre Co, PA
    Burial: 1843 in Howard Methodist Cemetery, Howard, Centre Co, PA

Citation: Michael Leyman, January 2, 1843, May 10, 1843, Copy of Will, Register of Wills, Centre County, PA.

Layman, Michael
    Will: January 02, 1843 in Howard Tp, Centre Co, PA

Source Title:	**Michael Leyman (con't)**
Citation:	Michael Leyman, Probate file, 2723, 9pp, microfiche, Centre Co, PA Reg of Wills, Bellefonte, PA, Norman Nicol, ndnicol@epix.net, Mar 2008.
	Layman, Michael
	Prob: Bet. May 10–June 08, 1843 in Centre Co, PA
	Will: January 02, 1843 in Howard Tp, Centre Co, PA
Source Title:	**Michael Lyman**
Citation:	Michael Lyman, List of Taxable Inhabitants, Centre Twp., 1810.
	Layman, Michael
	Occu: 1810; Trade
	Res: 1810 in Centre, Centre Co, PA
Citation:	Michael Lyman, Union Co, PA Tax list, 1796, Annals of Buffalo Valley, p 393.
	Layman, Michael
	Occu: 1796; Carpenter
Source Title:	**Michael Oberland**
Citation:	Michael Oberland, 1798, #3, York County Births 1730-1900, Humphrey, Gert Mysliwski,gert@foothill.net.
	Oberlander, Michael Baugher
	Birth: February 23, 1798 in Jefferson, Codorus, York Co, PA
Citation:	Michael Oberland, St. Matthews Lutheran Church records, Hanover, PA, Helda Kline.
	Oberlander, Michael Baugher
	Birth: February 23, 1798 in Jefferson, Codorus, York Co, PA
Source Title:	**Michael Oberlander**
Citation:	Michael Oberlander, findagrave.com.
	Oberlander, Michael Baugher
	Burial: Abt. 1880 in Saint Lukes Evangelical Lutheran Cemetery, New Bridgeville, PA
Source Title:	**Miller family information**
Citation:	Miller family information, Jean M. Sterner, Spring Grove, PA 17362.
	Hamm, Anna Maria
	Death: June 22, 1797 in York Co, PA
Citation:	Miller family information, Julie Azzalina, indyboy@email.msn.com.
	Hamm, Anna Maria
	Death: June 22, 1797 in York Co, PA
	Miller, Andrew
	Death: November 22, 1842 in Codorus, York Co, PA
Source Title:	**Miller Family information**
Citation:	Miller Family information, Jean M. Sterner, Spring Grove, PA 17362.
	Miller, Andrew
	Birth: March 14, 1752 in York Co, PA
	Death: November 22, 1842 in Codorus, York Co, PA
	Burial: 1842 in Emanuels (Jefferson) Union Cemetery, Jefferson, York Co, PA
	Miller, Maria Elizabeth
	Birth: October 17, 1777 in Cordorus, York Co, PA
	Werner, John George
	Burial: 1805 in St. Jacobs (Stone) Union, Glenville, York Co, PA
Source Title:	**Miller household**

Source Title: **Miller household (con't)**

Citation: Miller household, 1790 United States Census, York Co, PA, Roll M637 9, p 270, Image 0204, ancestry.com & Microfilm, PA State Library, Hbg, PA.

Miller, Andrew

Census: 1790 in Codorus, York Co, PA

Citation: Miller household, 1810 United States Census, York Co, PA, ancestry.com & Microfilm, PA State Library, Hbg, PA.

Miller, Andrew

Census: 1810 in Codorus, York Co, PA

Citation: Miller household, 1820 United States Census, York Co, PA, ancestry.com & Microfilm, PA State Library, Hbg, PA.

Miller, Andrew

Census: 1820 in Codorus, York Co, PA

Citation: Miller household, 1830 United States Census, York Co, PA, ancestry.com & Microfilm, PA State Library, Hbg, PA.

Miller, Andrew

Census: 1830 in Codorus, York Co, PA

Citation: Miller household, 1840 United States Census, York Co, PA, ancestry.com & Microfilm, PA State Library, Hbg, PA.

Miller, Andrew

Census: 1840 in Codorus, York Co, PA

Source Title: **Nail household**

Citation: Nail household, 1800 United States Census, Northumberland Co, PA, ancestry.com & Microfilm, PA State Library, Hbg, PA.

Neal, Henry

Census: 1800 in West Buffalo, Northumberland (Union) Co, PA

Source Title: **Neil household**

Citation: Neil household, 1790 United States Census, Mifflin, PA, ancestry.com & Microfilm, PA State Library, Hbg, PA.

Neal, Henry

Census: 1790 in Mifflin Co, PA

Source Title: **Nicholas Geib**

Citation: Nicholas Geib, Probate files, 1782, Rep 35, #436, York County Archives, York, PA, Deborah Hershey, Elizabethtown, PA, Dec 2008.

Geib, John Nicholas

Will: November 11, 1782 in Hellam, York Co, PA

Source Title: **Nicholas Geip, Sr**

Citation: Nicholas Geip, Sr., 1782, bk F, p 57, May 28, 1776, November 11, 1782, York County, PA Wills, 1749-1819, York County, PA, www.ancestry.com.

Geib, John Nicholas

Will: November 11, 1782 in Hellam, York Co, PA

Citation: Nicholas Geip, Sr., May 28, 1776, November 11, 1782, Will Abstracts of York County, PA, 1749-1819, Gert Mysliwski,gert@foothill.net.

Geib, John Nicholas

Will: November 11, 1782 in Hellam, York Co, PA

Source Title: **Nicholas Gype**

Citation: Nicholas Gype, Tax list, 1763, Hellam, York County, PA.

Geib, John Nicholas

Res: Bet. 1762–1763 in Hellam, York Co, PA

Source Title:	Nicholas Gype (con't)

Source Title: **Nicolas Geip Jr**

Citation: Nicolas Geip Jr, 1782, F-57, May 28, 1776, November 11, York County, PA Wills, 1749-1819, York County, PA, Gert Mysliwski,gert@foothill.net.

Geib, John Nicholas
Will: November 11, 1782 in Hellam, York Co, PA

Source Title: **Nicolas Gipe**

Citation: Nicolas Gipe, Tax list, 1762, Hellam, York County, PA.

Geib, John Nicholas
Res: Bet. 1762–1763 in Hellam, York Co, PA

Source Title: **Oberlander family information**

Citation: Oberlander family information, PA Births, Lebanon County, J. Humphrey.

Oberlander, Peter
Relgn: 1776; Heidelberg Church, Schaffertown, Lebanon Co, PA

Source Title: **Oberlander household**

Citation: Oberlander household, 1800 United States Census, York Co, PA, ancestry.com & Microfilm, PA State Library, Hbg, PA.

Oberlander, Michael Baugher
Census: 1800 in father; Manheim, York Co, PA w

Citation: Oberlander household, 1810 United States Census, York Co, PA, ancestry.com & Microfilm, PA State Library, Hbg, PA.

Oberlander, Michael Baugher
Census: 1810 in father; Shrewsburg, York Co, PA w

Citation: Oberlander household, 1830 United States Census, York Co, PA, ancestry.com & Microfilm, PA State Library, Hbg, PA.

Oberlander, Jacob Warner
Census: 1830 in father age 10; Upper Chanceford, York Co, PA w

Citation: Oberlander household, 1840 United States Census, York Co, PA, ancestry.com & Microfilm, PA State Library, Hbg, PA.

Oberlander, Jacob Warner
Census: 1840 in father age 10; Upper Chanceford, York Co, PA w

Citation: Oberlander household, 1850 United States Census, York Co, PA, ancestry.com & Microfilm, PA State Library, Hbg, PA.

Oberlander, Michael Baugher
Census: 1850 in Chanceford, York Co, PA

Citation: Oberlander household, 1850 United States Census, York Co, PA, ancestry.com & Microfilm, PA State Library, Hbg, PA.

Oberlander, Michael Baugher
Naturl:

Citation: Oberlander household, 1850 United States Census, York Co, PA, Roll M432 839, p 839, ancestry.com & Microfilm, PA State Library, Hbg, PA.

Oberlander, Jacob Warner
Occu: Bet. 1850–1880; Farmer

Citation: Oberlander household, 1850 United States Census, York Co, PA, Roll M432 839, p 839, ancestry.com & Microfilm, PA State Library, Hbg, PA.

Oberlander, Jacob Warner
Census: 1850 in Chanceford, York Co, PA

Citation: Oberlander household, 1860 United States Census, York Co, PA, ancestry.com & Microfilm, PA State Library, Hbg, PA.

Source Title: **Oberlander household (con't)**

Citation: Oberlander household, 1860 United States Census, York Co, PA, ancestry.com & Microfilm, PA State Library, Hbg, PA.

     Oberlander, Jacob Warner
         Propty: 1860 in $4000 + $640
          Occu: Bet. 1850–1880; Farmer
     Oberlander, Michael Baugher
          Occu: 1860; Laborer
         Propty: 1860 in $100

Citation: Oberlander household, 1860 United States Census, York Co, PA, ancestry.com & Microfilm, PA State Library, Hbg, PA.

     ?, Elizabeth
         Census: 1860 in Jac. Oberlander); Chanceford, York Co, PA (Kipe w
     Oberlander, Jacob Warner
         Census: 1860 in Chanceford, York Co, PA
     Oberlander, Michael Baugher
         Census: 1860 in Chanceford, York Co, PA

Citation: Oberlander household, 1870 United States Census, York Co, PA, ancestry.com & Microfilm, PA State Library, Hbg, PA.

     Gipe, Sarah "Sallie" Ann
          Occu: 1870; Keeping house
     Oberlander, Jacob Warner
          Propty: 1870 in $4000 + $1500
          Occu: Bet. 1850–1880; Farmer
     Overlander, Rebecca Jane
          Educ: 1870; School

Citation: Oberlander household, 1870 United States Census, York Co, PA, ancestry.com & Microfilm, PA State Library, Hbg, PA.

     Oberlander, Jacob Warner
         Census: 1870 in Chanceford, York Co, PA
     Oberlander, Michael Baugher
         Census: 1870 in Chanceford, York Co, PA
          Occu: 1870; Shoemaker

Citation: Oberlander household, 1870 United States Census, York Co, PA, Roll M593-1468, p 227, Image 67, ancestry.com & Microfilm, PA State Library, Hbg, PA.

     Overlander, Rebecca Jane
         Census: 1870 in Chanceford, York Co, PA (Rebeck)

Citation: Oberlander household, 1880 United States Census, York Co, PA, ancestry.com & Microfilm, PA State Library, Hbg, PA and 1880 United States Census, York Co, PA, FHL 1255207, Film T9-1207, p 599C, www.familysearch.org.

     Oberlander, Michael Baugher
          Occu: 1880; Home

Citation: Oberlander household, 1880 United States Census, York Co, PA, ancestry.com & Microfilm, PA State Library, Hbg, PA.

     Oberlander, Jacob Warner
         Census: 1880 in Chanceford, York Co, PA

Citation: Oberlander household, 1880 United States Census, York Co, PA, FHL 1255207, Film T9-1207, p 599C, www.familysearch.org.

     Oberlander, Jacob Warner
          Occu: Bet. 1850–1880; Farmer

Citation: Oberlander household, 1880 United States Census, York Co, PA, www.ancestry.com and 1880 United States Census, York Co, PA, FHL 1255207, Film T9-1207, p 599C, www.familysearch.org.

Source Title: **Oberlander household (con't)**

Citation: Oberlander household, 1880 United States Census, York Co, PA, www.ancestry.com and 1880 United States Census, York Co, PA, FHL 1255207, Film T9-1207, p 599C, www.familysearch.org.

Oberlander, Michael Baugher
    Census: 1880 in Chanceford, York Co, PA

Source Title: **Overland household**

Citation: Overland household, 1800 United States Census, York Co, PA, Roll M32 44, p 1351, Image 183, ancestry.com & Microfilm, PA State Library, Hbg, PA.

Oberlander, Jacob
    Census: 1800 in Manheim, York Co, PA (Overland)

Source Title: **Overlander household**

Citation: Overlander household, 1830 United States Census, York Co, PA, ancestry.com & Microfilm, PA State Library, Hbg, PA.

Oberlander, Michael Baugher
    Census: 1830 in Upper Chanceford, York Co, PA

Citation: Overlander household, 1840 United States Census, York Co, PA, ancestry.com & Microfilm, PA State Library, Hbg, PA.

Oberlander, Michael Baugher
    Census: 1840 in Chanceford, York Co, PA

Source Title: **Overlander-Baugher marriage**

Citation: Overlander-Baugher marriage, Hanover, PA, Christie Fleming, CFleming@eagle.org.

Baugher, Susan
    Marr: 1797 in Hanover, York Co, PA
Oberlander, Jacob
    Marr: 1797 in Hanover, York Co, PA

Source Title: **Overlander-Kipe marriage record**

Citation: Overlander-Kipe marriage record, #662-59, Calender of Vital Records of the Counties of York & Adams.

Gipe, Sarah "Sallie" Ann
    Marr: October 26, 1854 in St. Lukes (Stahleys) Lutheran, New Bridgeville, York Co, PA
Oberlander, Jacob Warner
    Marr: October 26, 1854 in St. Lukes (Stahleys) Lutheran, New Bridgeville, York Co, PA

Source Title: **Pedro Oberlander**

Citation: Pedro Oberlander, PA Census, 1772-1890, Philadelphia, PA, www.ancestry.com.

Oberlander, Peter
    Res: 1766 in Philadelphia, PA

Citation: Pedro Oberlander, Passenger and Immigration Lists Index, 1500-1900, myfamily.com, P. William Filby, ancestry.com.

Oberlander, Peter
    Immigr: 1766

Source Title: **Peter Klein**

Citation: Peter Klein, Abstract of Lancaster County Wills, Lancaster County Historical Society.

Klein, Peter Michael?
    Death: March 1806 in Manor Tp, Lancaster Co, PA

Source Title: **Peter Michael Klein**

Citation: Peter Michael Klein, Probate files, Bk I, Vol 1, p269, Archives Div, Lancaster Co Courthouse, Lancaster, PA.

Klein, Peter Michael?
> Death: March 1806 in Manor Tp, Lancaster Co, PA

Source Title: **Peter Oberlander**

Citation: Peter Oberlander, Probate files, loose files, Lancaster County Archives Division, Lancaster Co Courthouse, Lancaster, PA, Deborah Hershey, Elizabethtown, PA, Mar 2008.

Oberlander, Peter
> Death: December 28, 1780 in Heidelberg, Lancaster (Lebanon) Co, PA
> Prob: December 28, 1780 in Heidelberg, Lancaster Co, PA
> Will: May 01, 1777 in Heidelberg, Lancaster Co, PA

Source Title: **Peter Overlander**

Citation: Peter Overlander, World Tree, awt.ancestry.com/cgi-bin/sse.dll, www.ancestry.com.

Oberlander, Jacob
> Birth: 1768 in Berwick, York Co, PA
> Death: April 12, 1816 in Chanceford, York Co, PA

Oberlander, Peter
> Death: December 28, 1780 in Heidelberg, Lancaster (Lebanon) Co, PA

Source Title: **Rachel Leyman**

Citation: Rachel Leyman, Howard Cemetery, Centre Co, PA, p 5.

Neal, Rachel
> Death: December 23, 1855 in Howard, Centre Co, PA
> Burial: 1855 in Howard Methodist Cemetery, Howard, Centre Co, PA

Source Title: **Rebecca Layman**

Citation: Rebecca Layman, Pomfret Manor Cemetery, Sam Derr, Sunbury, PA, lot 130-B.

Overlander, Rebecca Jane
> Burial: November 23, 1921 in Pomfret Manor Cemetery, Sunbury, Northumberland Co, PA

Source Title: **Rebecca Lehman (Layman) death certificate**

Citation: Rebecca Lehman (Layman) death certificate, #105066, Reg # 456, #3457529, Novemrber 1921, Department of Vital Records, New Castle, PA.

Overlander, Rebecca Jane
> Res: 1921 in Weatherly, Carbon, PA
> Death: November 20, 1921 in Hazleton State Hospital, Hazleton, Luzerne Co, PA
> Burial: November 23, 1921 in Pomfret Manor Cemetery, Sunbury, Northumberland Co, PA
> CasDth: Pneumonia, Labor
> Funeral: 1921 in P? Manor, Weatherly, Carbon, PA

Source Title: **Rieman household**

Citation: Rieman household, 1820 United States Census, York Co, PA, ancestry.com & Microfilm, PA State Library, Hbg, PA.

Reiman, John
> Census: 1820 in West Manchester, York Co, PA

Source Title: **Sallie Duncan**

Source Title: **Sallie Duncan (con't)**

Citation: Sallie Duncan, Cemetery record, Apr 1933, A genealogists Guide to Burials in Northumberland Co, PA, Vol I, Meiser & Meiser, 1989.

Duncan, Sarah "Sallie"
      Birth: March 14, 1872 in Sunbury, Northumberland Co, PA
      Death: February 03, 1915 in Sunbury, Northumberland Co, PA

Source Title: **Sarah Duncan**

Citation: Sarah Duncan, Baptisms of Infants, Zion Evan Luth Register, 1851-1892, Sunbury, PA, p41.

Duncan, Sarah "Sallie"
      Birth: March 14, 1872 in Sunbury, Northumberland Co, PA

Source Title: **Sarah Oberlander**

Citation: Sarah Oberlander, Probate files, 1874, Rep 42, Bk 342, York County Archives, York, PA, Deborah Hershey, Elizabethtown, PA, Dec 2008.

Gipe, Sarah "Sallie" Ann
      Will: November 25, 1874 in Chanceford, York Co, PA

Citation: Sarah Oberlander, Probate files, 1874, Rep 42, York County Archives, York, PA, Deborah Hershey, Elizabethtown, PA, Dec 2008.

Gipe, Sarah "Sallie" Ann
      Death: December 20, 1874 in Chanceford, York Co, PA
      Prob: March 24, 1875 in Chanceford, York Co, PA

Source Title: **Warner family information**

Citation: Warner family information, JWerner.txt, Don Varner, DRVarner@aol.com.

?, Judith
      Birth: March 1746
      Death: January 12, 1829 in Codorus, York Co, PA
Miller, Maria Elizabeth
      Birth: October 17, 1777 in Cordorus, York Co, PA
Warner, John Christian
      Birth: October 24, 1775 in York Co, PA
      Death: 1842 in York Co, PA
      Baptism: November 19, 1775 in St. Jacobs (Stone) Union, Glenville, York Co, PA
Warner, Maria Catherine
      Birth: March 21, 1798 in Hanover, York Co, PA
Werner, John George
      Birth: February 23, 1754 in PA
      Death: August 16, 1805 in Codorus, York Co, PA
      Immigr: Abt. 1755; Germany to USA (ship Brother)

Source Title: **Warner household**

Citation: Warner household, 1790 United States Census, York Co, PA, Roll M637 9, p 284, Image 0221, ancestry.com & Microfilm, PA State Library, Hbg, PA.

Werner, John George
      Census: 1790 in York Co, PA

Citation: Warner household, 1800 United States Census, York Co, PA, ancestry.com & Microfilm, PA State Library, Hbg, PA.

Warner, Maria Catherine
      Census: 1800 in father; Codorus, York Co, PA w

Citation: Warner household, 1810 United States Census, York Co, PA, ancestry.com & Microfilm, PA State Library, Hbg, PA.

Source Title: **Warner household (con't)**

Citation: Warner household, 1810 United States Census, York Co, PA, ancestry.com & Microfilm, PA State Library, Hbg, PA.

Warner, Maria Catherine

Census: 1810 in father; Codorus, York Co, PA w

Citation: Warner household, 1810 United States Census, York Co, PA, Roll M252 57, p 207, Image 218, ancestry.com & Microfilm, PA State Library, Hbg, PA.

Warner, John Christian

Census: 1810 in Codorus, York Co, PA

Citation: Warner household, 1820 United States Census, York Co, PA, ancestry.com & Microfilm, PA State Library, Hbg, PA.

Warner, John Christian

Census: 1820 in Peach Bottom, York Co, PA

Citation: Warner household, 1830 United States Census, York Co, PA, ancestry.com & Microfilm, PA State Library, Hbg, PA.

Warner, John Christian

Census: 1830 in Upper Chanceford, York Co, PA

Citation: Warner household, 1840 United States Census, York Co, PA, ancestry.com & Microfilm, PA State Library, Hbg, PA.

Warner, John Christian

Census: 1840 in Chanceford, York Co, PA

Citation: Warner household, 1850 United States Census, York Co, PA, ancestry.com & Microfilm, PA State Library, Hbg, PA.

Miller, Maria Elizabeth

Census: 1850 in son Jacob; Chanceford, York Co, PA w

Source Title: **Willard household**

Citation: Willard household, 1920 United States Census, Northumberland Co, PA, Roll T625 1611, p 7A, ED 134, Image 0913, ancestry.com & Microfilm, PA State Library, Hbg, PA.

Duncan, Irvin Wilfred

Census: 1920 in Sunbury, Northumberland Co, PA

Layman, Charlotte "Lottie" Virginia

Census: 1920 in Sunbury, Northumberland Co, PA (Willard)

Citation: Willard household, 1920 United States Census, Northumberland Co, PA, Roll T625 1611, p 7A, ED 134, Image 0913, ancestry.com & Microfilm, PA State Library, Hbg, PA.

Duncan, Irvin Wilfred

Educ: 1920; School

Res: 1920 in 920 Susquehanna Ave., Sunbury, Northumberland Co, PA

Layman, Charlotte "Lottie" Virginia

Res: Bet. 1920–1930 in 920 Susquehanna Ave., Sunbury, Northumberland Co, PA

Citation: Willard household, 1930 United States Census, Northumberland Co, PA, Roll T626 2091, p 7A, ED 71, Image 0681, ancestry.com & Microfilm, PA State Library, Hbg, PA.

Layman, Charlotte "Lottie" Virginia

Census: 1930 in Sunbury, Northumberland Co, PA (Willard)

Citation: Willard household, 1930 United States Census, Northumberland Co, PA, Roll T626 2091, p 7A, ED 71, Image 0681, ancestry.com & Microfilm, PA State Library, Hbg, PA.

Layman, Charlotte "Lottie" Virginia

Res: Bet. 1920–1930 in 920 Susquehanna Ave., Sunbury, Northumberland Co, PA

Source Title: **William Bager**

Citation: William Bager, World Tree, awt.ancestry.com/cgi-bin/sse.dll, www.ancestry.com.

Source Title:	**William Bager (con't)**
Citation:	William Bager, World Tree, awt.ancestry.com/cgi-bin/sse.dll, www.ancestry.com.
	Bager, John George William
	Birth: April 15, 1750 in Simmern, Rhineland-Palatinate, Germany
	Kepner, Eva Catherine
	Death: March 11, 1803 in Berwick, York Co, PA
Source Title:	**William Bauger**
Citation:	William Bauger, April 18, 1798, May 17, 1798, Probate Invent. Index York County, PA, 1749-1850, Berwick, Adams Co County, PA, Gert gert@foothill.net.
	Bager, John George William
	Will: May 17, 1798 in Berwick, York Co, PA
Source Title:	**William Duncan**
Citation:	William Duncan, April 1978, PA, Social Security Death Index, www.familysearch.org.
	Duncan, Irvin Wilfred
	Birth: November 27, 1901 in Sunbury, Northumberland Co, PA
Citation:	William Duncan, Baptisms of Infants, Zion Evan Luth Register, 1851-1892, Sunbury, PA, p41.
	Duncan, William
	Baptism: September 29, 1876 in Zion Evangelical Lutheran Church, Sunbury, Northumberland Co, PA
Citation:	William Duncan, Northumberland Co County, Pennsylvania, 1851-92, Zion Evangelical Church, www.ancestry.com.
	Duncan, William
	Baptism: September 29, 1876 in Zion Evangelical Lutheran Church, Sunbury, Northumberland Co, PA
Citation:	William Duncan, Pomfret Manor Cemetery, Sam Derr, Sunbury, PA, lot 130-B.
	Duncan, William
	Burial: September 14, 1906 in Pomfret Manor Cemetery, Sunbury, Northumberland Co, PA
Citation:	William Duncan, Pomfret Manor Cemetery, Sunbury, Northumberland Co, PA, NCHS, The Hunter House, Sunbury, PA.
	Duncan, William
	Birth: January 18, 1876 in Sunbury, Northumberland Co, PA
Citation:	William Duncan, Probate files, July 1906, Northumberland County Courthouse, Reg of Wills, Bk 12, p424, Sunbury, PA, Robyn Jackson, genealogylover@msn.com, 2008.
	Duncan, William
	Prob: September 17, 1906 in Sunbury, Northumberland Co, PA
	Will: July 24, 1906 in Sunbury, Northumberland Co, PA
Source Title:	**Wm Baugher**
Citation:	Wm Baugher, September 9, 1775, Land record, #11766, Berwick, York Co, PA.
	Bager, John George William
	Res: Bet. 1775–1788 in Berwick, York Co, PA
Source Title:	**Wm Duncan**
Citation:	Wm Duncan, Northumberland Co County Courthouse, Register of Wills, 11-27-1901.
	Duncan, William
	Occu: 1901; Laborer
	Res: 1901 in 918 Susquehanna Ave., Sunbury, Northumberland, PA
Source Title:	**Wm Duncan death certificate**

Source Title: **Wm Duncan death certificate (con't)**

Citation: Wm Duncan death certificate, #0030852, #90924, Northumberland Co, PA, Department of Vital records, New Castle, PA.

Duncan, William

       Occu: 1906; Machinist

       Res: 1906 in 920 Susquehanna Ave., Sunbury, Northumberland Co, PA

       Birth: January 16, 1876 in Sunbury, Northumberland Co, PA

       Death: September 11, 1906 in Sunbury, Northumberland Co, PA

       CasDth: Pulmonary tuberculosis

       Funeral: 1906 in J. Hartman, Sunbury, Northumberland Co, PA

Citation: Wm Duncan death certificate, #0030852, #90924, Northumberland Co, PA, Department of Vital records, New Castle, PA.

Duncan, William

       Burial: September 14, 1906 in Pomfret Manor Cemetery, Sunbury, Northumberland Co, PA

Source Title: **Wolliam (sic) Baugher**

Citation: Wolliam (sic) Baugher, April 18, 1798, May 17, 1798, Will Abstracts of York County, PA, 1749-1819, Gert Mysliwski,gert@foothill.net.

Bager, John George William

       Will: May 17, 1798 in Berwick, York Co, PA

Afterword

Without my ancestors, I would have been had the chance to experience the wonders of life. Thank you grandma and grandpa, you have allowed me to see beautiful places, do wonderful things and meet amazing people. This is my testament.

About the Author

Marc D. Thompson delved into writing and genealogy at a very early age. He wrote stories, poems, lyrics and family history books. Marc went on to write and research in high school and college, earning a BS degree from Moravian College. He has presented genealogical lectures and authored seven family history volumes and recently published *The Fitness Book of Lists* and *Virtual Personal Training Manual*. His other published works include numerous genealogical books and a poetry compilation, with poetic appearances in Fighting Chance Magazine, Love's Chance Magazine, Northern Stars Magazine, Offerings, Poetry Motel, Suzerian Enterprises and The Pink Chameleon.

Thompson currently pens a monthly genealogy blog and a fitness blog at ideafit.com. He.is a member of the Association of Professional Genealogists and founded a PA Genealogy Society. He was the County Coordinator of the Chatham Co, GA USGenweb site and wrote a monthly genealogy column for Atlantic Avenue Magazine. Writing now for over four decades, when he puts pen to paper, eloquent, heat-felt yet real-life truths emerge. He has been influenced by science, art and his relationships, and yet at the same time marvels at the cosmically-driven direction he receives from energy around him. Thompson believes in what he calls Creatalytical Thinking: The fusion of creativity and analysis to view life more fully and fulfill his place in this world.

MARC D. THOMPSON, VIRTUFIT.NET™

www.VirtuFit.net - marc@VirtuFit.net - skype: VirtuFit

ideafit: www.ideafit.com/profile/marc-d-thompson

Index of Individuals

Index of Individuals

Index of Individuals

Index of Individuals